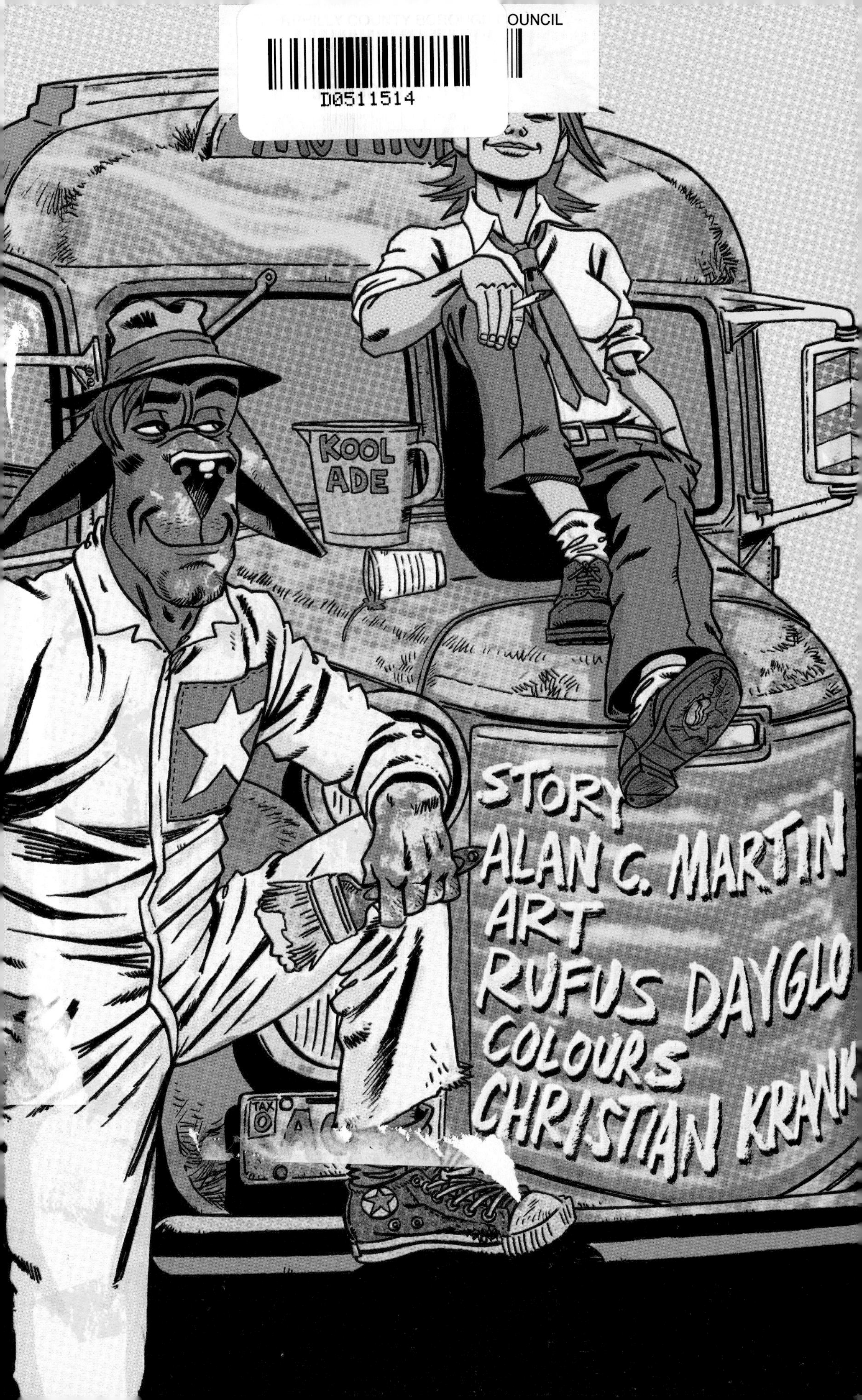
KOOL
ADE
STORY
ALAN C. MARTIN
ART
RUFUS DAYGLO
COLOURS
CHRISTIAN KRANK

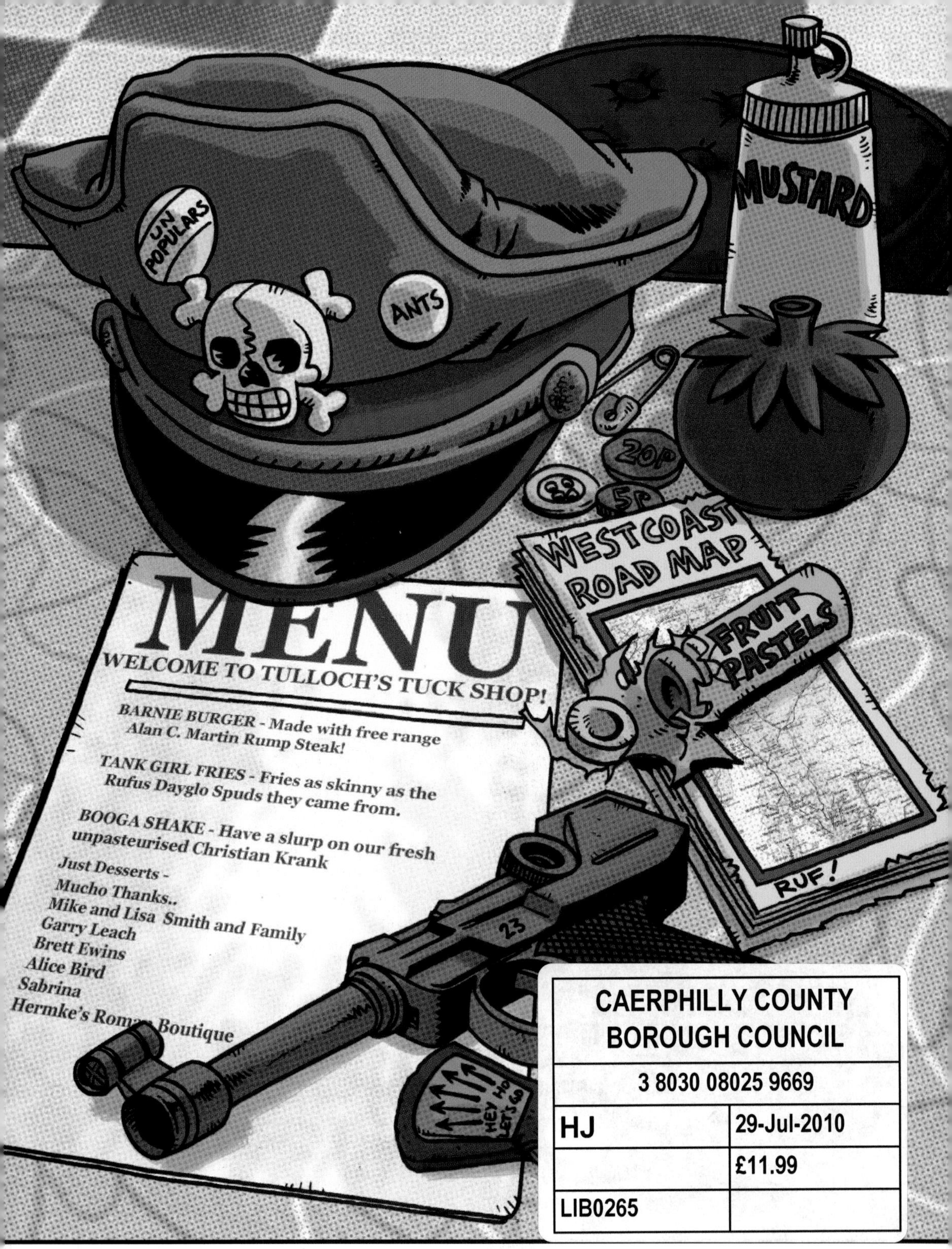
UN POPULARS
ANTS
MUSTARD
20p
5p
WESTCOAST ROAD MAP
FRUIT PASTELS
MENU
WELCOME TO TULLOCH'S TUCK SHOP!
BARNIE BURGER - Made with free range Alan C. Martin Rump Steak!
TANK GIRL FRIES - Fries as skinny as the Rufus Dayglo Spuds they came from.
BOOGA SHAKE - Have a slurp on our fresh unpasteurised Christian Krank
Just Desserts -
Mucho Thanks..
Mike and Lisa Smith and Family
Garry Leach
Brett Ewins
Alice Bird
Sabrina
Hermke's Rom... Boutique
23
RUF!
HEY HO LET'S GO

Tank Girl: Visions of Booga

ISBN: 9781848561663

Tank Girl created by Alan Martin and Jamie Hewlett.

Published by Titan Books, a division of Titan Publishing Group Ltd., 144 Southwark Street, London SE1 0UP. First published by IDW Publishing as *Tank Girl: Visions of Booga* #1-4. No portion of this book may be reproduced or transmitted, in any form or by any mans, without the express written permission of the copyright holder. A CIP catalogue record for this book is available from the British Library.

Printed in Italy.
First printing: November 2008
10 9 8 7 6 5 4 3 2 1

Written by: **Alan Martin**
Art by: **Rufus Dayglo**
Colours by: **Christian Krank**
Letters by: **Chris Mowry**
Edits by: **Denton J. Tipton**
Covers by: **Ashley Wood**

Visit our website: www.titanbooks.com

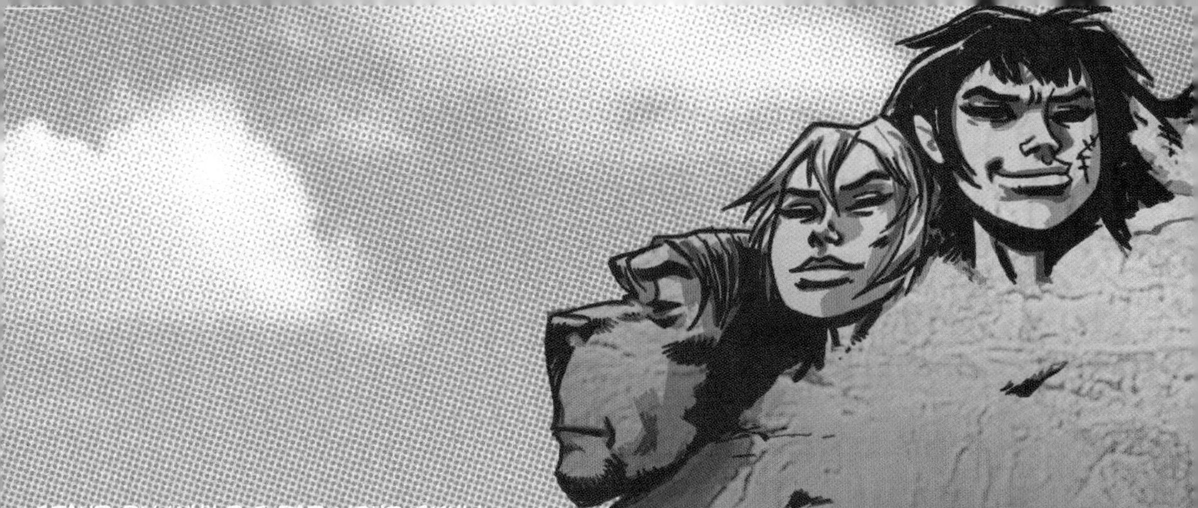

STAND BY WHILE I PAD YOUR SKULL...

THE ORIGINAL INSPIRATION FOR *VISIONS OF BOOGA* CAME AFTER A VIEWING OF BILLY WILDER'S *SOME LIKE IT HOT.* I WANTED TO PITCH TANK GIRL AND BOOGA AGAINST THE WORLD WITHOUT A PENNY TO THEIR NAME (WHICH WAS ALWAYS MY FAVOURITE OPENING IN LAUREL AND HARDY'S FILMS), AND HAVE THEM TRAVEL ACROSS A CONTINENT TO ESCAPE THE CLUTCHES OF THE EVIL MOB. ONCE THEY WERE OUT ON THE ROAD, I COULDN'T HELP MY OLD PERENNIAL INSPIRATIONS OF THE BEAT GENERATION AND EARLY HIPPYDOM FILTERING INTO THE MIX, SO THINGS STARTED TO WARP A LITTLE FROM THERE ON IN.

ULTIMATELY THE VISIONS THAT BOOGA BRINGS ABOUT BY READING THE MYSTICAL OLD BEAT GENERATION BOOK OUT LOUD ARE NOTHING MORE THAN THE QUESTIONS THAT WERE ARISING IN MY MIND AS I WAS WRITING IT ("WHY AM I WRITING THIS?", " IS STORY JUST COMMENTARY OR IS IT LIFE CHANGING? WORLD CHANGING?", " OR IS MY JOB TO SUPPLY A CERTAIN SMALL SECTION OF SOCIETY WITH THE SATISFACTION THAT SOMEONE OUT THERE CAN RELATE TO THE STRANGE THOUGHTS IN THEIR HEADS?") WHEN I SHOULD HAVE BEEN FOCUSING ON THE PLOT, CHARACTERIZATION AND STORY TWISTS THAT WOULD HAVE DELIVERED ANSWERS TO ALL THE ABOVE.

THAT SAID, I THINK THE FINAL PIECE WORKS VERY WELL AS A WHOLE - FAR SLOWER AND MORE DOWNBEAT THAN TANK GIRL HAS EVER BEEN BEFORE, AND SOMEHOW DELIVERING INSIGHT AND PATHOS IN ITS OWN RIDICULOUS WAY.

RUFUS REALLY GOT HIS TEETH INTO THIS ONE, AT LAST GIVEN THE CHANCE TO EVOLVE HIS OWN TAKE ON TANK GIRL WITH BRILLIANT STYLE AND PANACHE, WITH FINAL FLOURISHES FROM WUNDERKIND COLOURIST CHRISTIAN PUTTING A GREAT BIG CHERRY ON THE CAKE (I LOVE HOW THE STARK, COLD BLUENESS OF THE EAST COAST AT THE START OF THE STORY SLOWLY MORPHS INTO THE RICH SUN-DRENCHED SATURATION OF THE WEST COAST IN THE FINAL PAGES).

I HOPE YOU ENJOY *VISIONS OF BOOGA*, IT'S ALREADY ONE OF MY PERSONAL FAVOURITES.

PLANT YOU NOW, DIG YOU LATER.

ALAN C. MARTIN

THE RED SQUIRREL HIDE
PAXTON HOUSE
BERWICKSHIRE
AUGUST 2008

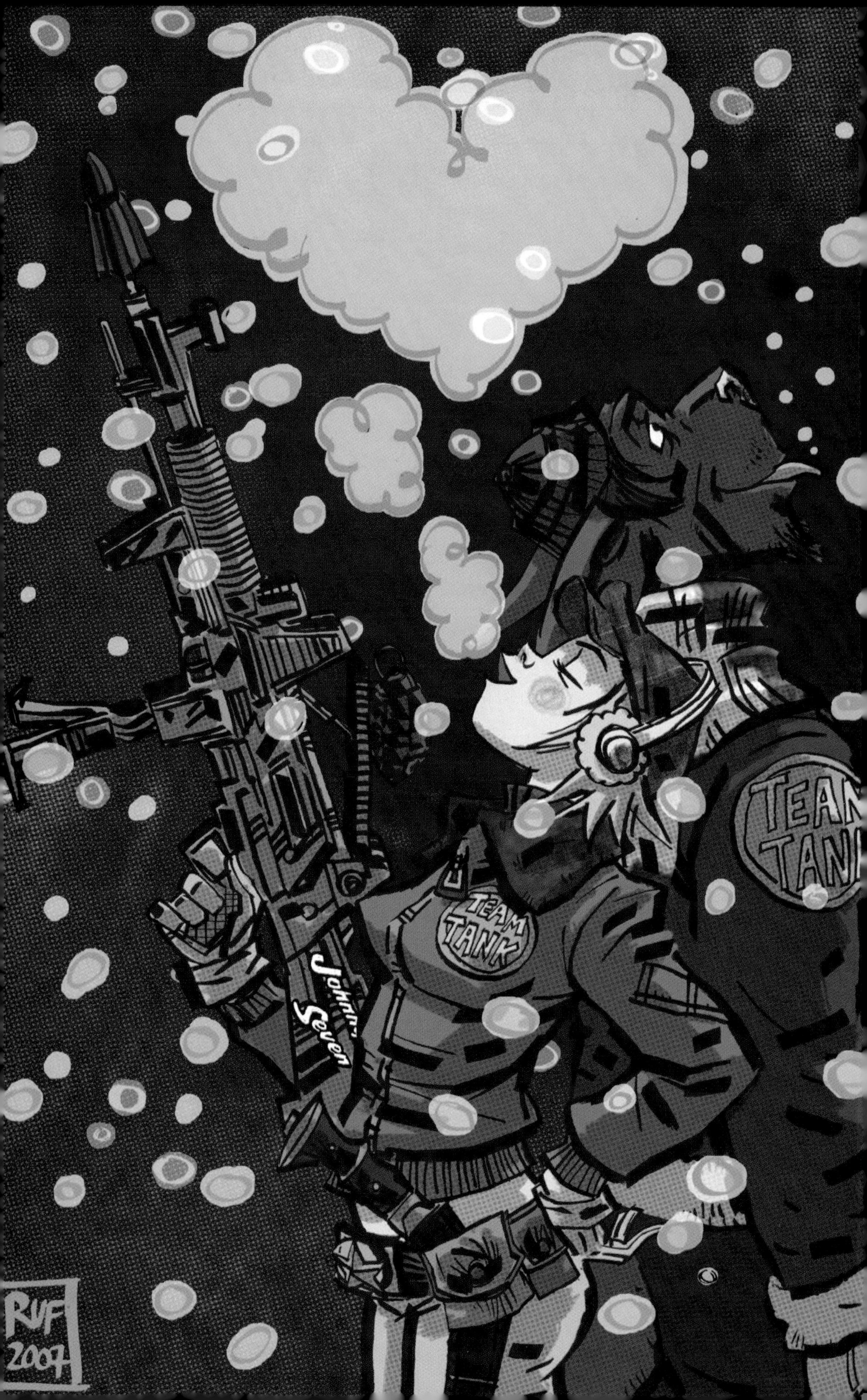
TEAM TANK
Seven
RUF 2007

TANK GIRL

A FEISTY, SEXY, ANGRY, OVERLY FASHION CONSCIOUS, RENEGADE TANK-PILOT WITH A PARTICULARLY BENT SENSE OF HUMOUR. SHE LEFT THE ARMY SOME TIME AGO AND TOOK THEIR BEST TANK WITH HER.

FAVOURITE FILM: *GODZILLA VS MOTHRA.*

FAVOURITE LP: *THE ROLLING STONES – THEIR SATANIC MAJESTIES REQUEST.*

LIKES: KIDNEY BEANS.

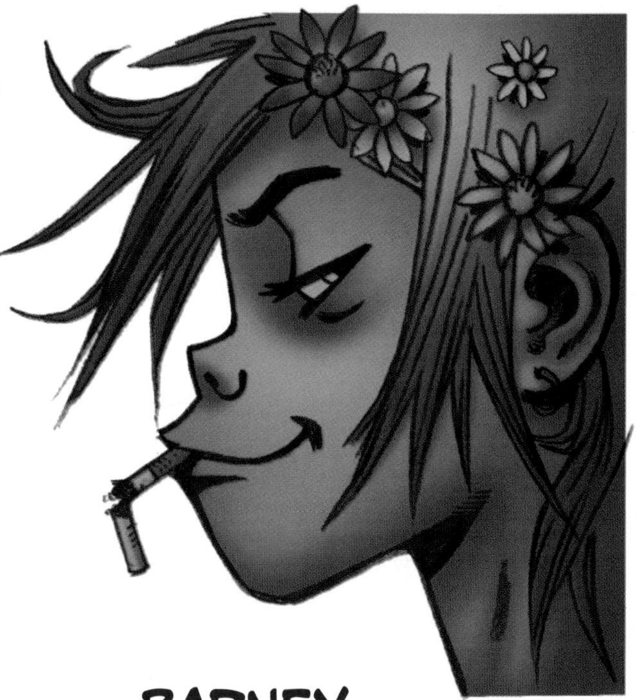

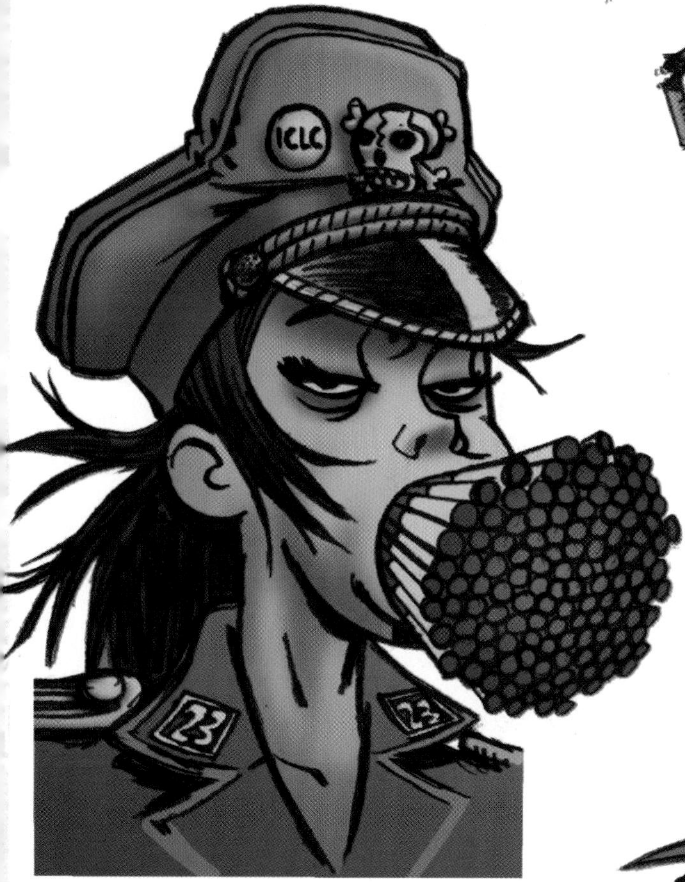
ICLC
23
23

BARNEY

AN ESCAPED MENTAL PATIENT. OSTENSIBLY A PRETTY, CUDDLY, AND CHARMING GIRL, SHE CAN SUDDENLY TURN INTO A DANGEROUS PSYCHOPATH. TANK GIRL LIKES TO KEEP HER AROUND TO ADD A CERTAIN "SPICE" TO HER LIFE.

FAVOURITE FILM: *STAR TREK 3: THE SEARCH FOR SPOCK.*

FAVOURITE LP: *MUD – MUD ROCK.*

LIKES: CLAMBAKES.

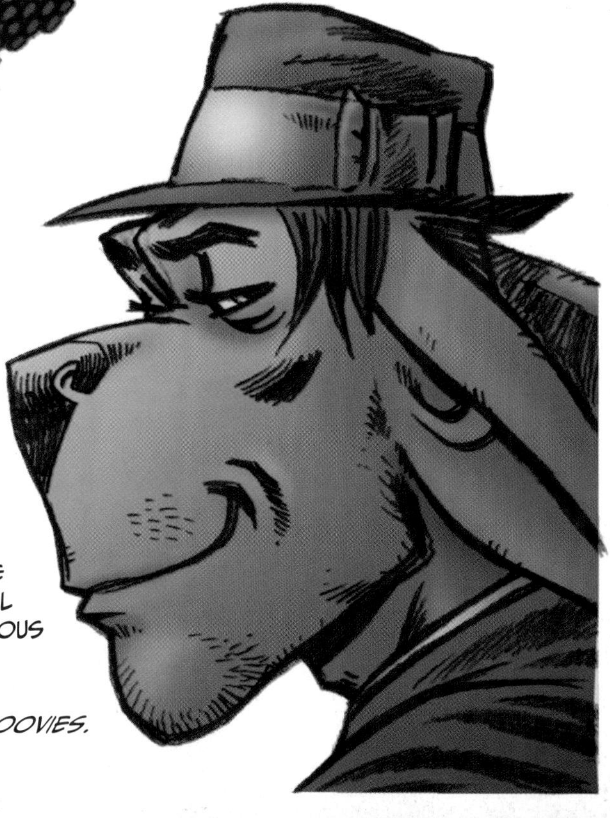

BOOGA

TANK GIRL'S DOPEY KANGAROO BOYFRIEND. MOVED INTO THE TANK ONE DAY WITHOUT BEING INVITED AND HAS STAYED EVER SINCE. OFTEN THE BUTT OF TANK GIRL'S JOKES, HE IS ALWAYS WELL MEANING AND EAGER TO JOIN IN ON ANY RIDICULOUS SCHEME THAT COMES HIS WAY.

FAVOURITE FILM: *SOME KIND OF WONDERFUL.*

FAVOURITE LP: *TEENAGE HEAD – THE FLAMIN' GROOVIES.*

LIKES: SOFT PYJAMAS.

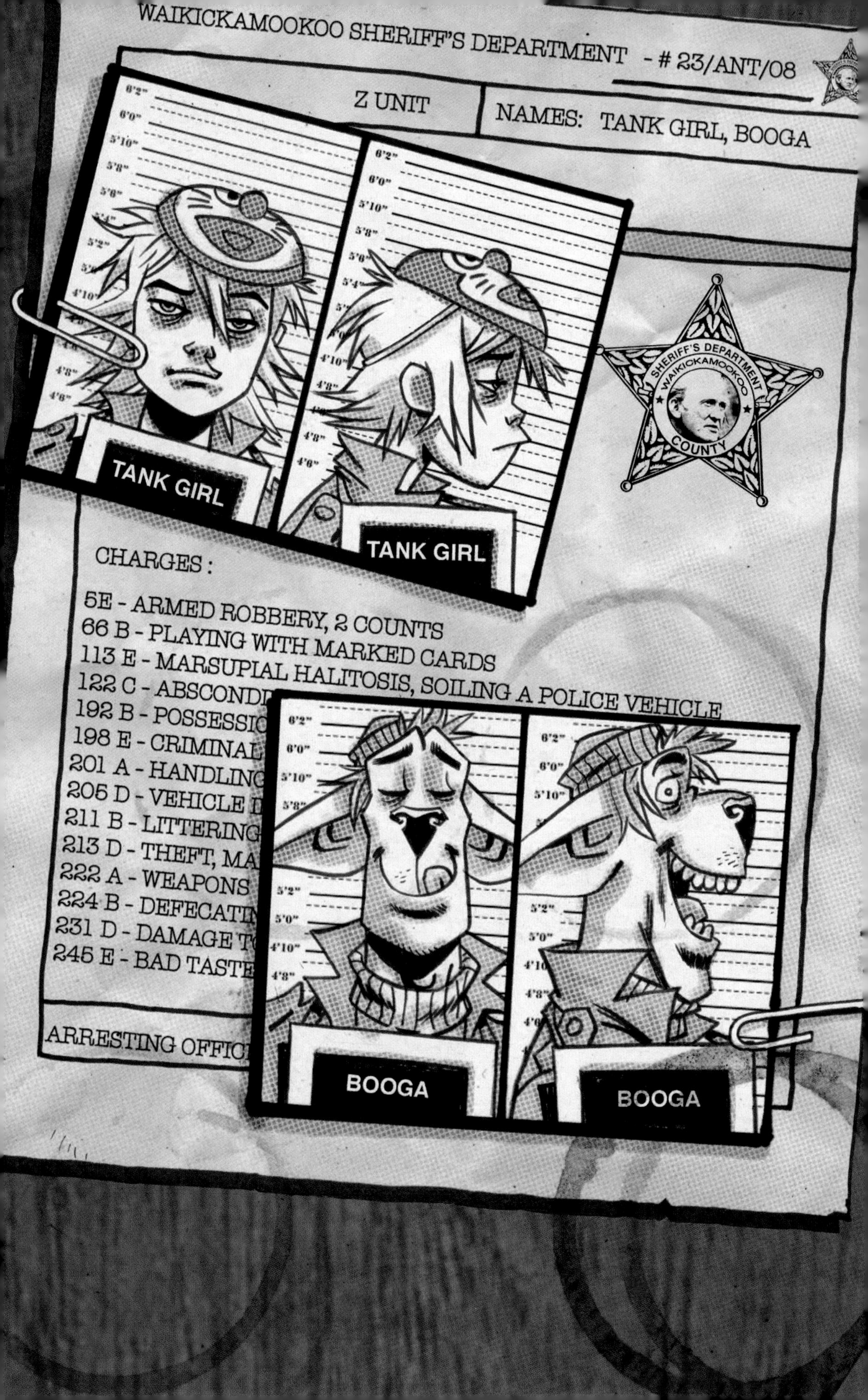
WAIKICKAMOOKOO SHERIFF'S DEPARTMENT - # 23/ANT/08
Z UNIT
NAMES: TANK GIRL, BOOGA
TANK GIRL
TANK GIRL
SHERIFF'S DEPARTMENT WAIKICKAMOOKOO COUNTY
CHARGES :
5E - ARMED ROBBERY, 2 COUNTS
66 B - PLAYING WITH MARKED CARDS
113 E - MARSUPIAL HALITOSIS, SOILING A POLICE VEHICLE
122 C - ABSCOND
192 B - POSSESSIO
198 E - CRIMINAL
201 A - HANDLIN
205 D - VEHICLE
211 B - LITTERING
213 D - THEFT, MA
222 A - WEAPONS
224 B - DEFECATI
231 D - DAMAGE T
245 E - BAD TASTE
ARRESTING OFFIC
BOOGA
BOOGA

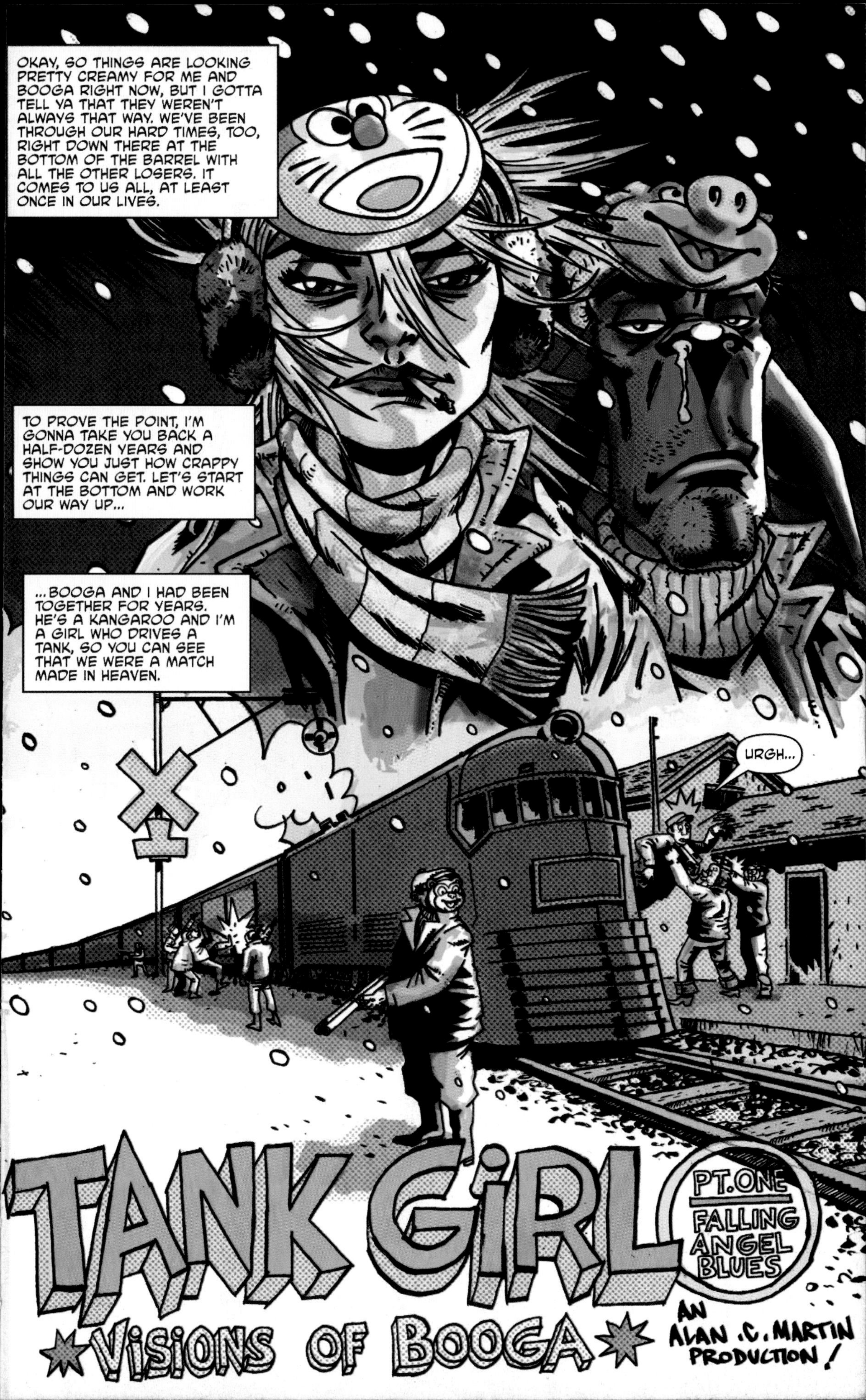

OKAY, SO THINGS ARE LOOKING PRETTY CREAMY FOR ME AND BOOGA RIGHT NOW, BUT I GOTTA TELL YA THAT THEY WEREN'T ALWAYS THAT WAY. WE'VE BEEN THROUGH OUR HARD TIMES, TOO, RIGHT DOWN THERE AT THE BOTTOM OF THE BARREL WITH ALL THE OTHER LOSERS. IT COMES TO US ALL, AT LEAST ONCE IN OUR LIVES.
TO PROVE THE POINT, I'M GONNA TAKE YOU BACK A HALF-DOZEN YEARS AND SHOW YOU JUST HOW CRAPPY THINGS CAN GET. LET'S START AT THE BOTTOM AND WORK OUR WAY UP...
...BOOGA AND I HAD BEEN TOGETHER FOR YEARS. HE'S A KANGAROO AND I'M A GIRL WHO DRIVES A TANK, SO YOU CAN SEE THAT WE WERE A MATCH MADE IN HEAVEN.
URGH...
TANK GIRL
PT. ONE
FALLING ANGEL BLUES
VISIONS OF BOOGA
AN ALAN .C. MARTIN PRODUCTION!

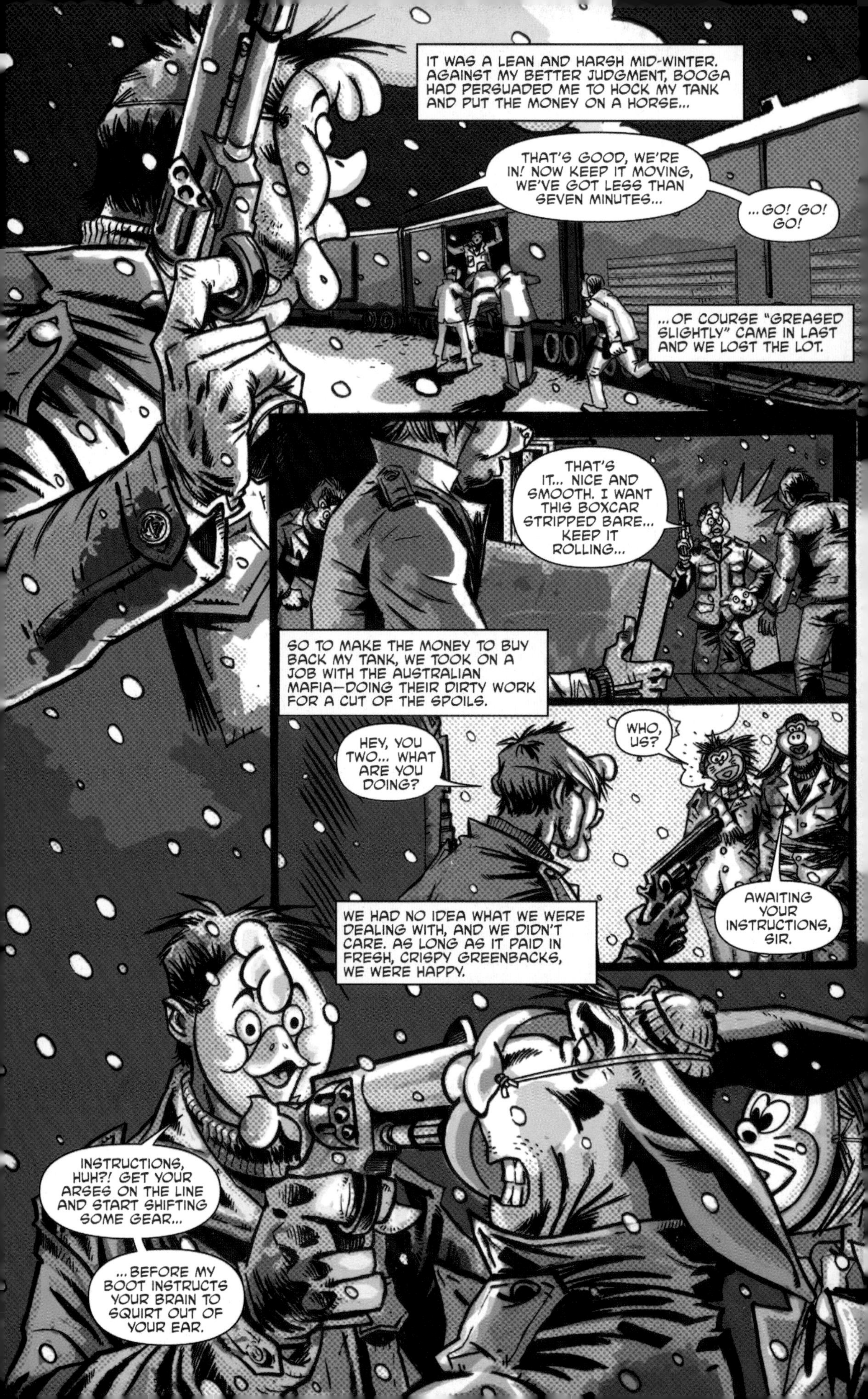
IT WAS A LEAN AND HARSH MID-WINTER. AGAINST MY BETTER JUDGMENT, BOOGA HAD PERSUADED ME TO HOCK MY TANK AND PUT THE MONEY ON A HORSE...
THAT'S GOOD, WE'RE IN! NOW KEEP IT MOVING, WE'VE GOT LESS THAN SEVEN MINUTES...
...GO! GO! GO!
...OF COURSE "GREASED SLIGHTLY" CAME IN LAST AND WE LOST THE LOT.
THAT'S IT... NICE AND SMOOTH. I WANT THIS BOXCAR STRIPPED BARE... KEEP IT ROLLING...
SO TO MAKE THE MONEY TO BUY BACK MY TANK, WE TOOK ON A JOB WITH THE AUSTRALIAN MAFIA—DOING THEIR DIRTY WORK FOR A CUT OF THE SPOILS.
HEY, YOU TWO... WHAT ARE YOU DOING?
WHO, US?
AWAITING YOUR INSTRUCTIONS, SIR.
WE HAD NO IDEA WHAT WE WERE DEALING WITH, AND WE DIDN'T CARE. AS LONG AS IT PAID IN FRESH, CRISPY GREENBACKS, WE WERE HAPPY.
INSTRUCTIONS, HUH?! GET YOUR ARSES ON THE LINE AND START SHIFTING SOME GEAR...
...BEFORE MY BOOT INSTRUCTS YOUR BRAIN TO SQUIRT OUT OF YOUR EAR.

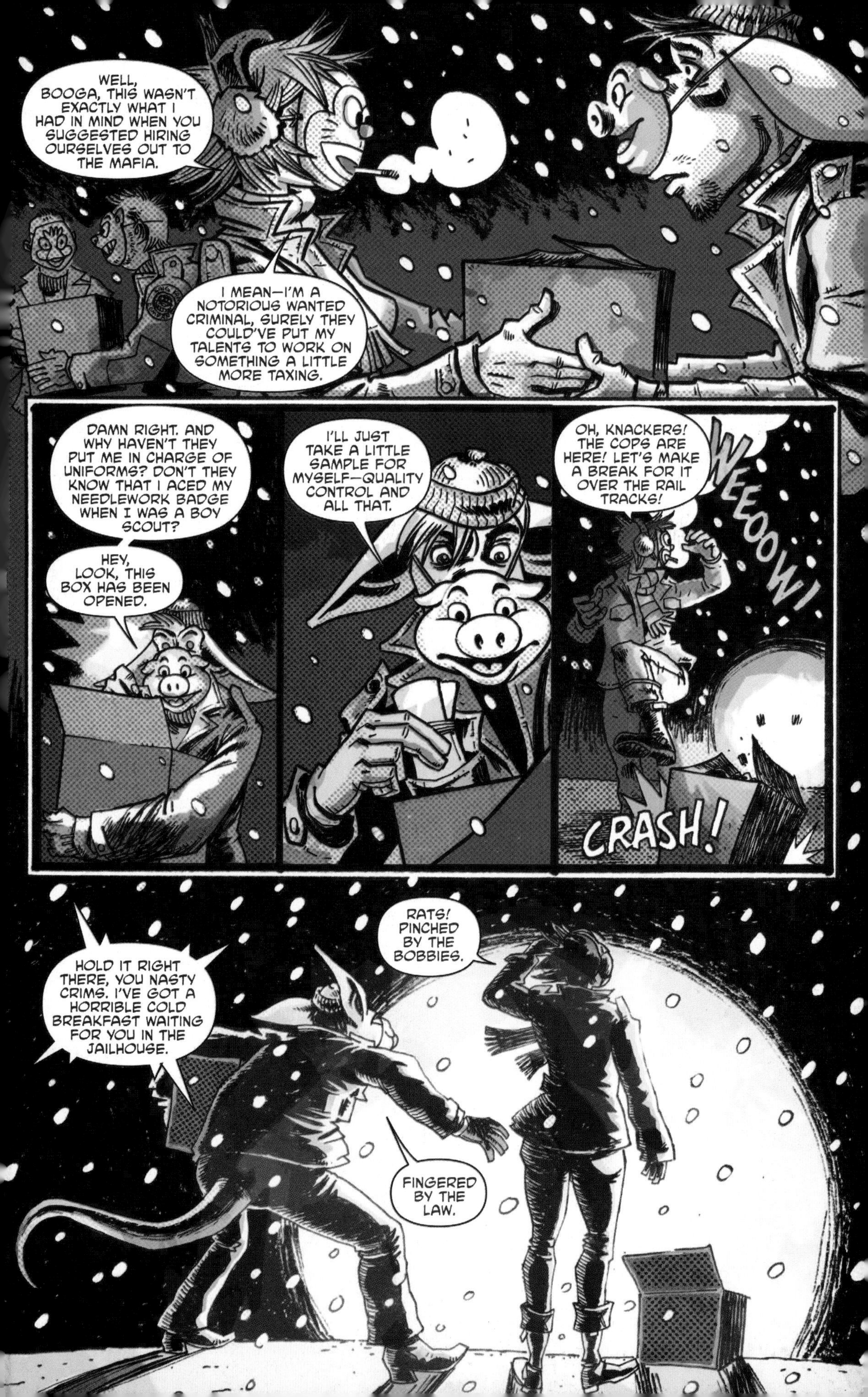
WELL, BOOGA, THIS WASN'T EXACTLY WHAT I HAD IN MIND WHEN YOU SUGGESTED HIRING OURSELVES OUT TO THE MAFIA.
I MEAN—I'M A NOTORIOUS WANTED CRIMINAL, SURELY THEY COULD'VE PUT MY TALENTS TO WORK ON SOMETHING A LITTLE MORE TAXING.
DAMN RIGHT. AND WHY HAVEN'T THEY PUT ME IN CHARGE OF UNIFORMS? DON'T THEY KNOW THAT I ACED MY NEEDLEWORK BADGE WHEN I WAS A BOY SCOUT?
HEY, LOOK, THIS BOX HAS BEEN OPENED.
I'LL JUST TAKE A LITTLE SAMPLE FOR MYSELF—QUALITY CONTROL AND ALL THAT.
OH, KNACKERS! THE COPS ARE HERE! LET'S MAKE A BREAK FOR IT OVER THE RAIL TRACKS!
WEEOOOW!
CRASH!
HOLD IT RIGHT THERE, YOU NASTY CRIMS. I'VE GOT A HORRIBLE COLD BREAKFAST WAITING FOR YOU IN THE JAILHOUSE.
RATS! PINCHED BY THE BOBBIES.
FINGERED BY THE LAW.

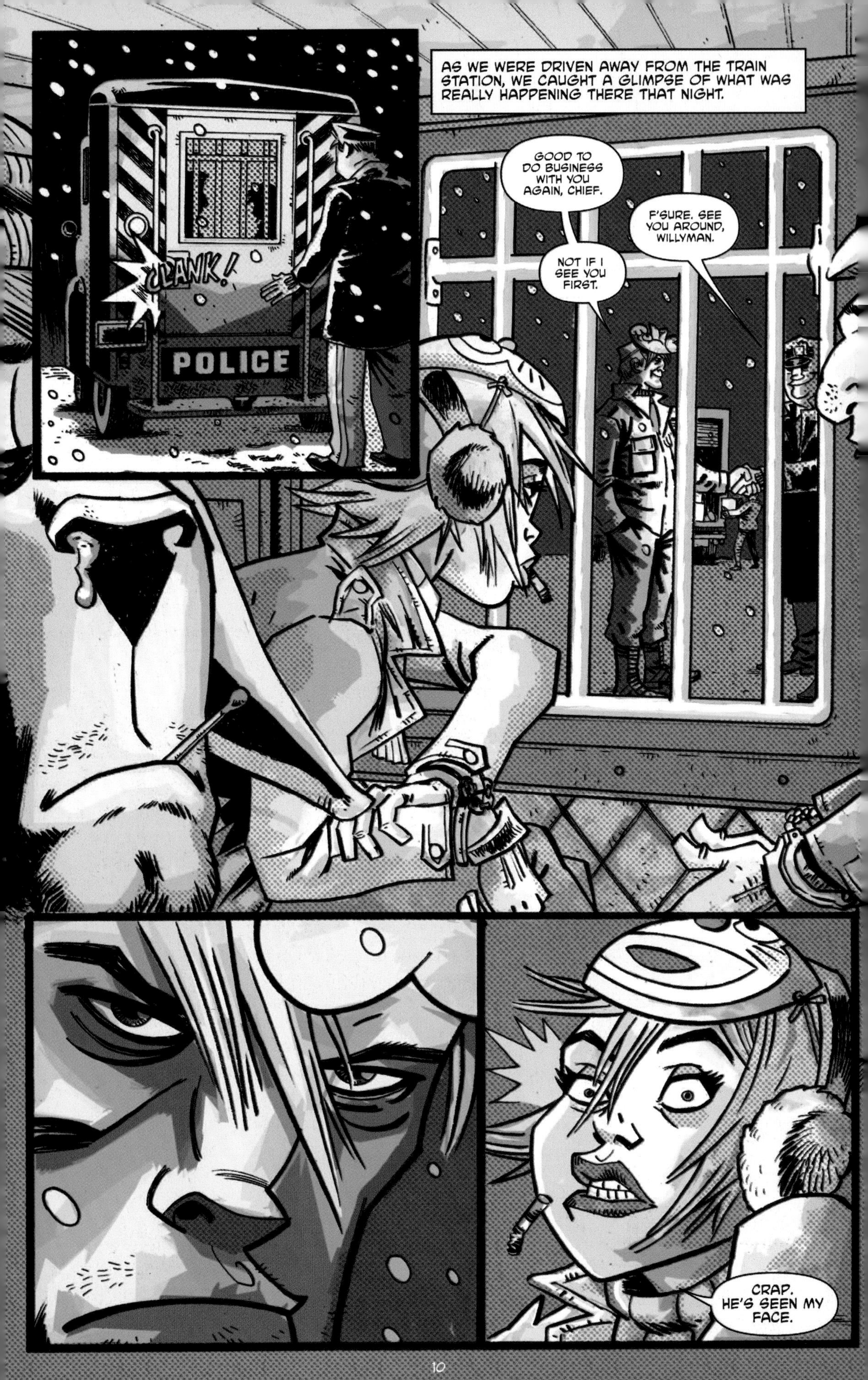
CLANK!
POLICE
AS WE WERE DRIVEN AWAY FROM THE TRAIN STATION, WE CAUGHT A GLIMPSE OF WHAT WAS REALLY HAPPENING THERE THAT NIGHT.
GOOD TO DO BUSINESS WITH YOU AGAIN, CHIEF.
F'SURE. SEE YOU AROUND, WILLYMAN.
NOT IF I SEE YOU FIRST.
CRAP. HE'S SEEN MY FACE.

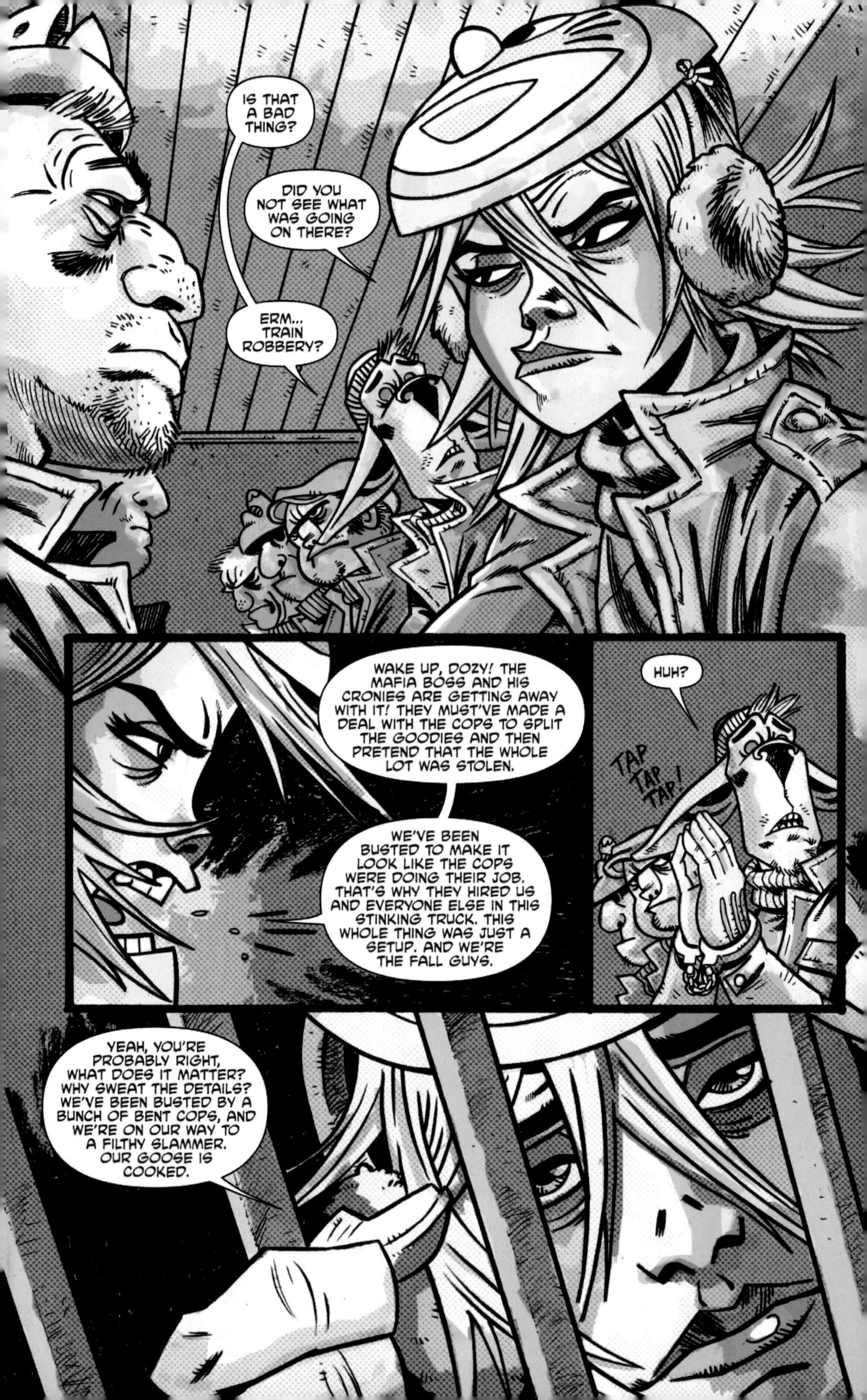
IS THAT A BAD THING?
DID YOU NOT SEE WHAT WAS GOING ON THERE?
ERM... TRAIN ROBBERY?
WAKE UP, DOZY! THE MAFIA BOSS AND HIS CRONIES ARE GETTING AWAY WITH IT! THEY MUST'VE MADE A DEAL WITH THE COPS TO SPLIT THE GOODIES AND THEN PRETEND THAT THE WHOLE LOT WAS STOLEN.
WE'VE BEEN BUSTED TO MAKE IT LOOK LIKE THE COPS WERE DOING THEIR JOB. THAT'S WHY THEY HIRED US AND EVERYONE ELSE IN THIS STINKING TRUCK. THIS WHOLE THING WAS JUST A SETUP. AND WE'RE THE FALL GUYS.
HUH?
TAP TAP TAP!
YEAH, YOU'RE PROBABLY RIGHT, WHAT DOES IT MATTER? WHY SWEAT THE DETAILS? WE'VE BEEN BUSTED BY A BUNCH OF BENT COPS, AND WE'RE ON OUR WAY TO A FILTHY SLAMMER. OUR GOOSE IS COOKED.

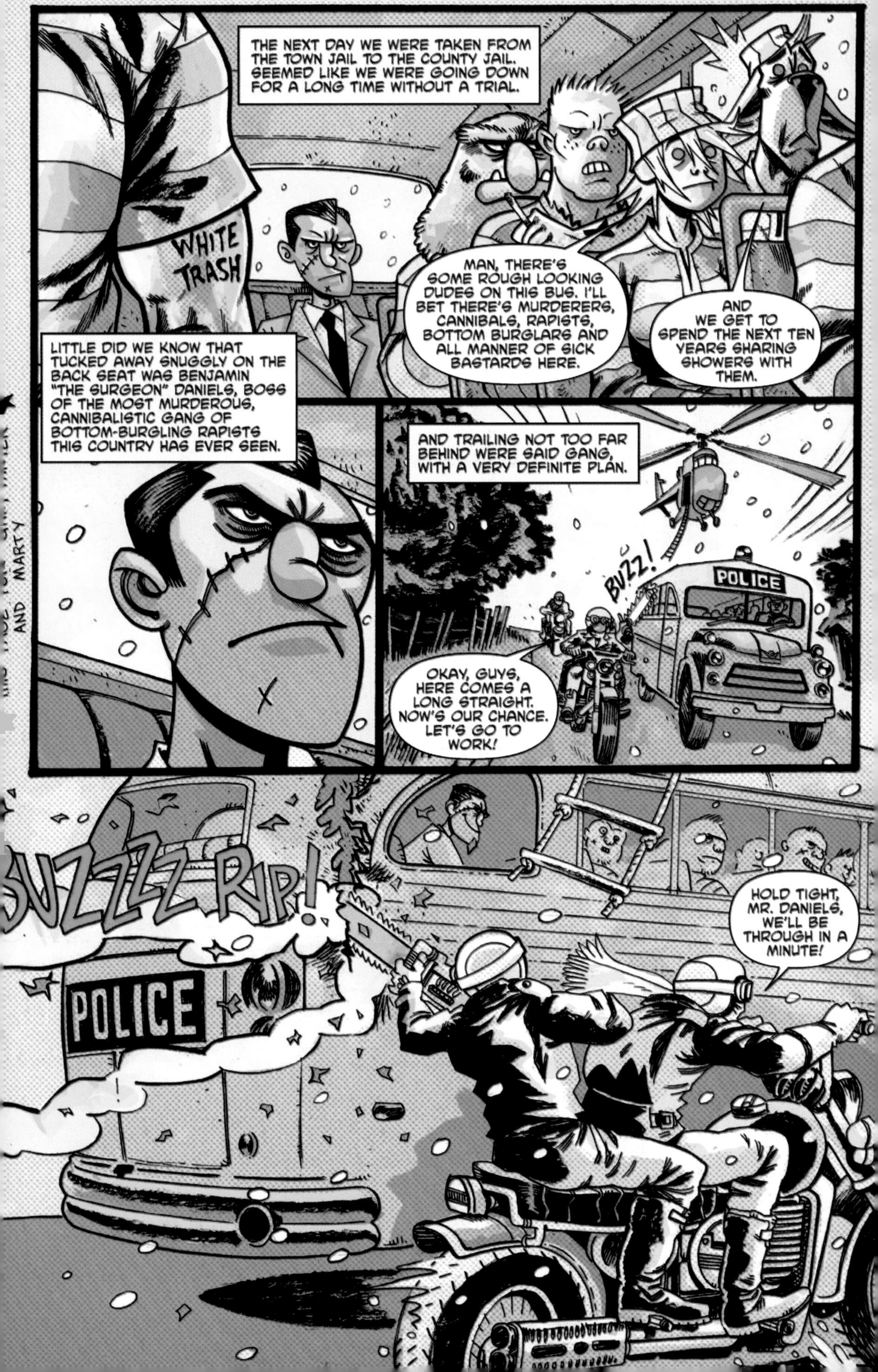
THE NEXT DAY WE WERE TAKEN FROM THE TOWN JAIL TO THE COUNTY JAIL. SEEMED LIKE WE WERE GOING DOWN FOR A LONG TIME WITHOUT A TRIAL.
WHITE TRASH
MAN, THERE'S SOME ROUGH LOOKING DUDES ON THIS BUS. I'LL BET THERE'S MURDERERS, CANNIBALS, RAPISTS, BOTTOM BURGLARS AND ALL MANNER OF SICK BASTARDS HERE.
AND WE GET TO SPEND THE NEXT TEN YEARS SHARING SHOWERS WITH THEM.
LITTLE DID WE KNOW THAT TUCKED AWAY SNUGGLY ON THE BACK SEAT WAS BENJAMIN "THE SURGEON" DANIELS, BOSS OF THE MOST MURDEROUS, CANNIBALISTIC GANG OF BOTTOM-BURGLING RAPISTS THIS COUNTRY HAS EVER SEEN.
AND TRAILING NOT TOO FAR BEHIND WERE SAID GANG, WITH A VERY DEFINITE PLAN.
BUZZ!
POLICE
OKAY, GUYS, HERE COMES A LONG STRAIGHT. NOW'S OUR CHANCE. LET'S GO TO WORK!
BUZZZZ RIP!
POLICE
HOLD TIGHT, MR. DANIELS, WE'LL BE THROUGH IN A MINUTE!

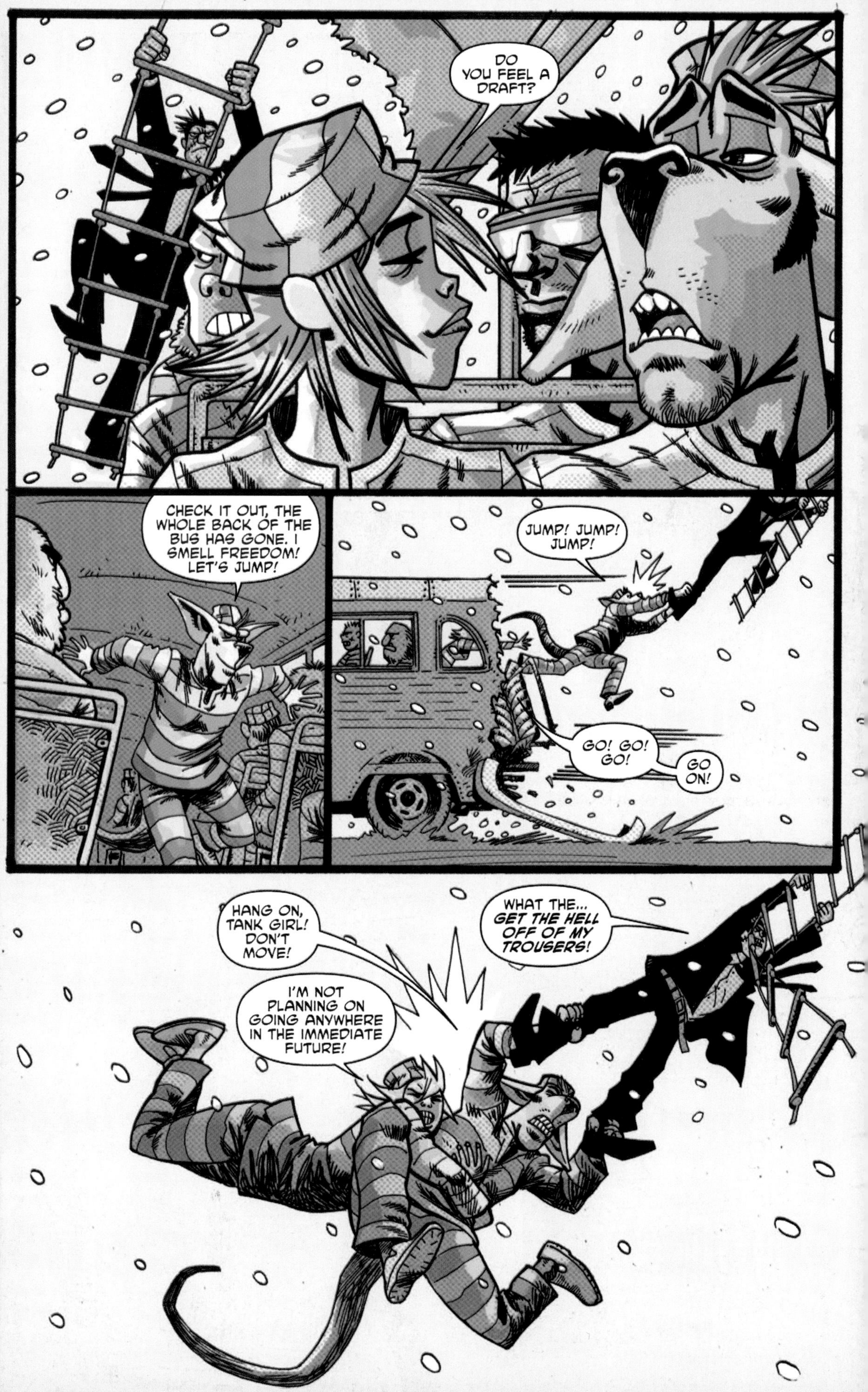
DO YOU FEEL A DRAFT?
CHECK IT OUT, THE WHOLE BACK OF THE BUS HAS GONE. I SMELL FREEDOM! LET'S JUMP!
JUMP! JUMP! JUMP!
GO! GO! GO!
GO ON!
HANG ON, TANK GIRL! DON'T MOVE!
WHAT THE... GET THE HELL OFF OF MY TROUSERS!
I'M NOT PLANNING ON GOING ANYWHERE IN THE IMMEDIATE FUTURE!

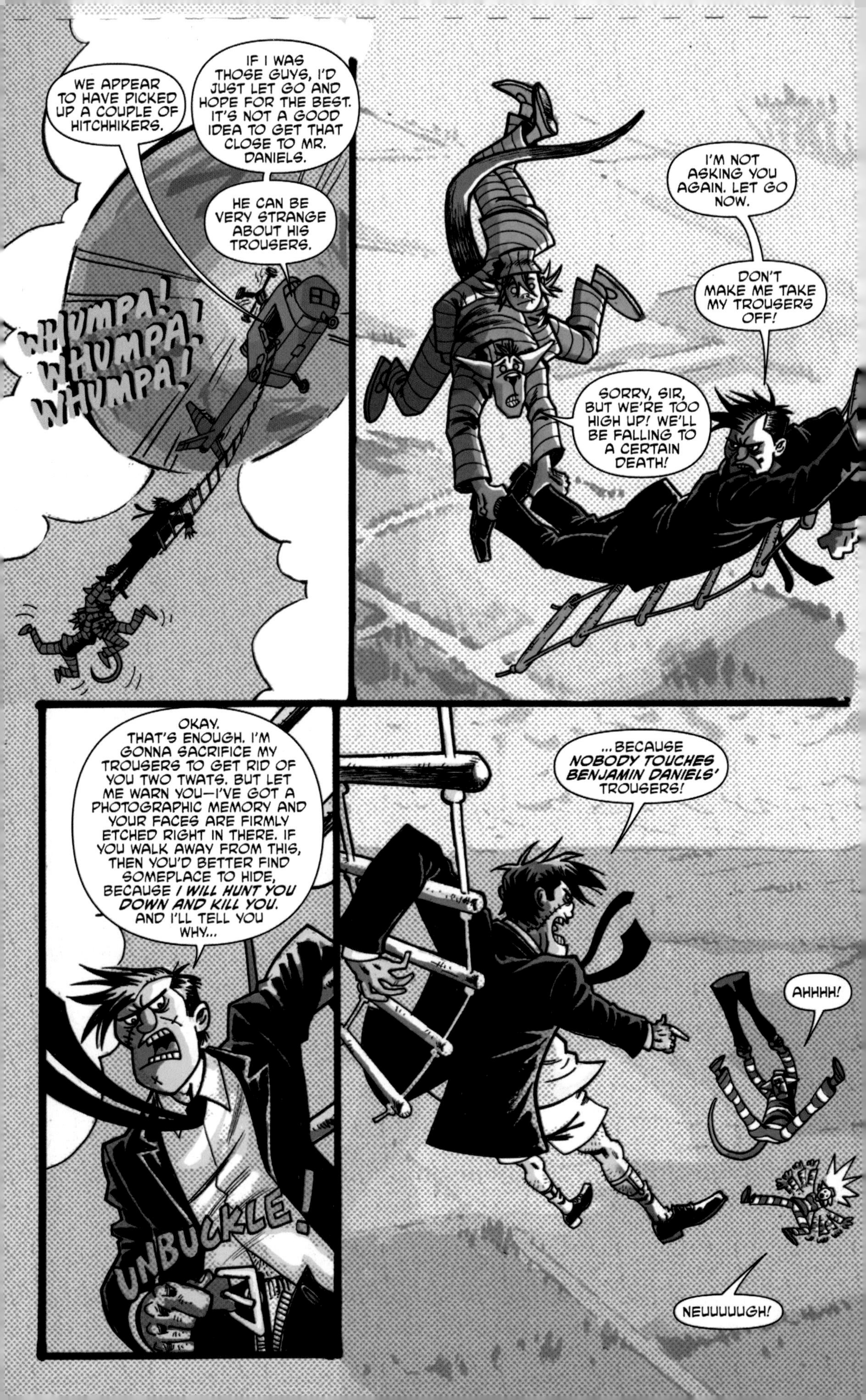
WE APPEAR TO HAVE PICKED UP A COUPLE OF HITCHHIKERS.
IF I WAS THOSE GUYS, I'D JUST LET GO AND HOPE FOR THE BEST. IT'S NOT A GOOD IDEA TO GET THAT CLOSE TO MR. DANIELS.
HE CAN BE VERY STRANGE ABOUT HIS TROUSERS.
WHUMPA! WHUMPA! WHUMPA!
I'M NOT ASKING YOU AGAIN. LET GO NOW.
DON'T MAKE ME TAKE MY TROUSERS OFF!
SORRY, SIR, BUT WE'RE TOO HIGH UP! WE'LL BE FALLING TO A CERTAIN DEATH!
OKAY. THAT'S ENOUGH. I'M GONNA SACRIFICE MY TROUSERS TO GET RID OF YOU TWO TWATS. BUT LET ME WARN YOU—I'VE GOT A PHOTOGRAPHIC MEMORY AND YOUR FACES ARE FIRMLY ETCHED RIGHT IN THERE. IF YOU WALK AWAY FROM THIS, THEN YOU'D BETTER FIND SOMEPLACE TO HIDE, BECAUSE *I WILL HUNT YOU DOWN AND KILL YOU.* AND I'LL TELL YOU WHY...
UNBUCKLE!
...BECAUSE *NOBODY TOUCHES BENJAMIN DANIELS'* TROUSERS!
AHHHH!
NEUUUUUGH!

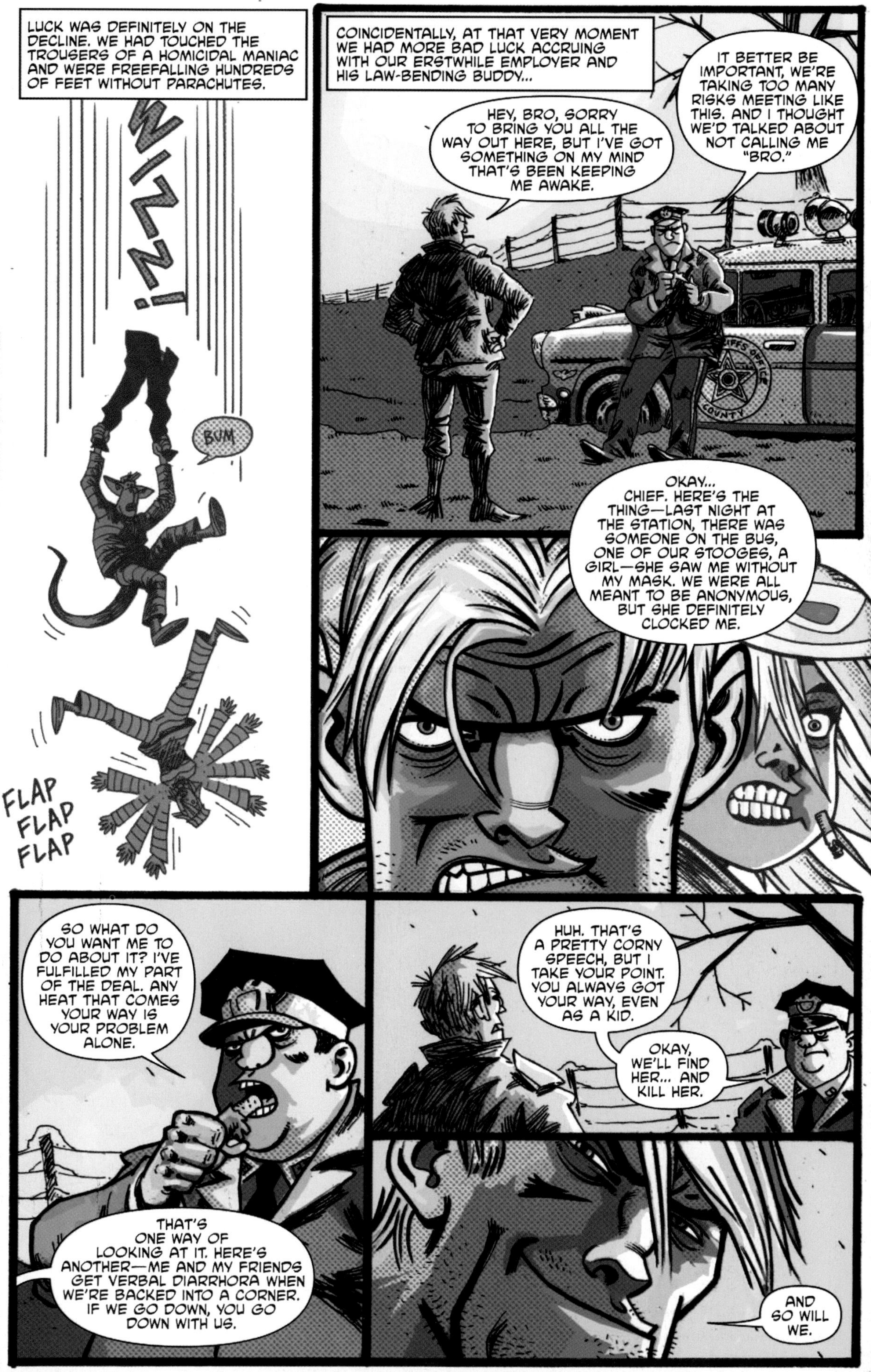
LUCK WAS DEFINITELY ON THE DECLINE. WE HAD TOUCHED THE TROUSERS OF A HOMICIDAL MANIAC AND WERE FREEFALLING HUNDREDS OF FEET WITHOUT PARACHUTES.
WIZZZ!
BUM
FLAP FLAP FLAP
COINCIDENTALLY, AT THAT VERY MOMENT WE HAD MORE BAD LUCK ACCRUING WITH OUR ERSTWHILE EMPLOYER AND HIS LAW-BENDING BUDDY...
HEY, BRO, SORRY TO BRING YOU ALL THE WAY OUT HERE, BUT I'VE GOT SOMETHING ON MY MIND THAT'S BEEN KEEPING ME AWAKE.
IT BETTER BE IMPORTANT, WE'RE TAKING TOO MANY RISKS MEETING LIKE THIS. AND I THOUGHT WE'D TALKED ABOUT NOT CALLING ME "BRO."
OKAY... CHIEF. HERE'S THE THING—LAST NIGHT AT THE STATION, THERE WAS SOMEONE ON THE BUS, ONE OF OUR STOOGES, A GIRL—SHE SAW ME WITHOUT MY MASK. WE WERE ALL MEANT TO BE ANONYMOUS, BUT SHE DEFINITELY CLOCKED ME.
SO WHAT DO YOU WANT ME TO DO ABOUT IT? I'VE FULFILLED MY PART OF THE DEAL. ANY HEAT THAT COMES YOUR WAY IS YOUR PROBLEM ALONE.
THAT'S ONE WAY OF LOOKING AT IT. HERE'S ANOTHER—ME AND MY FRIENDS GET VERBAL DIARRHORA WHEN WE'RE BACKED INTO A CORNER. IF WE GO DOWN, YOU GO DOWN WITH US.
HUH. THAT'S A PRETTY CORNY SPEECH, BUT I TAKE YOUR POINT. YOU ALWAYS GOT YOUR WAY, EVEN AS A KID.
OKAY, WE'LL FIND HER... AND KILL HER.
AND SO WILL WE.

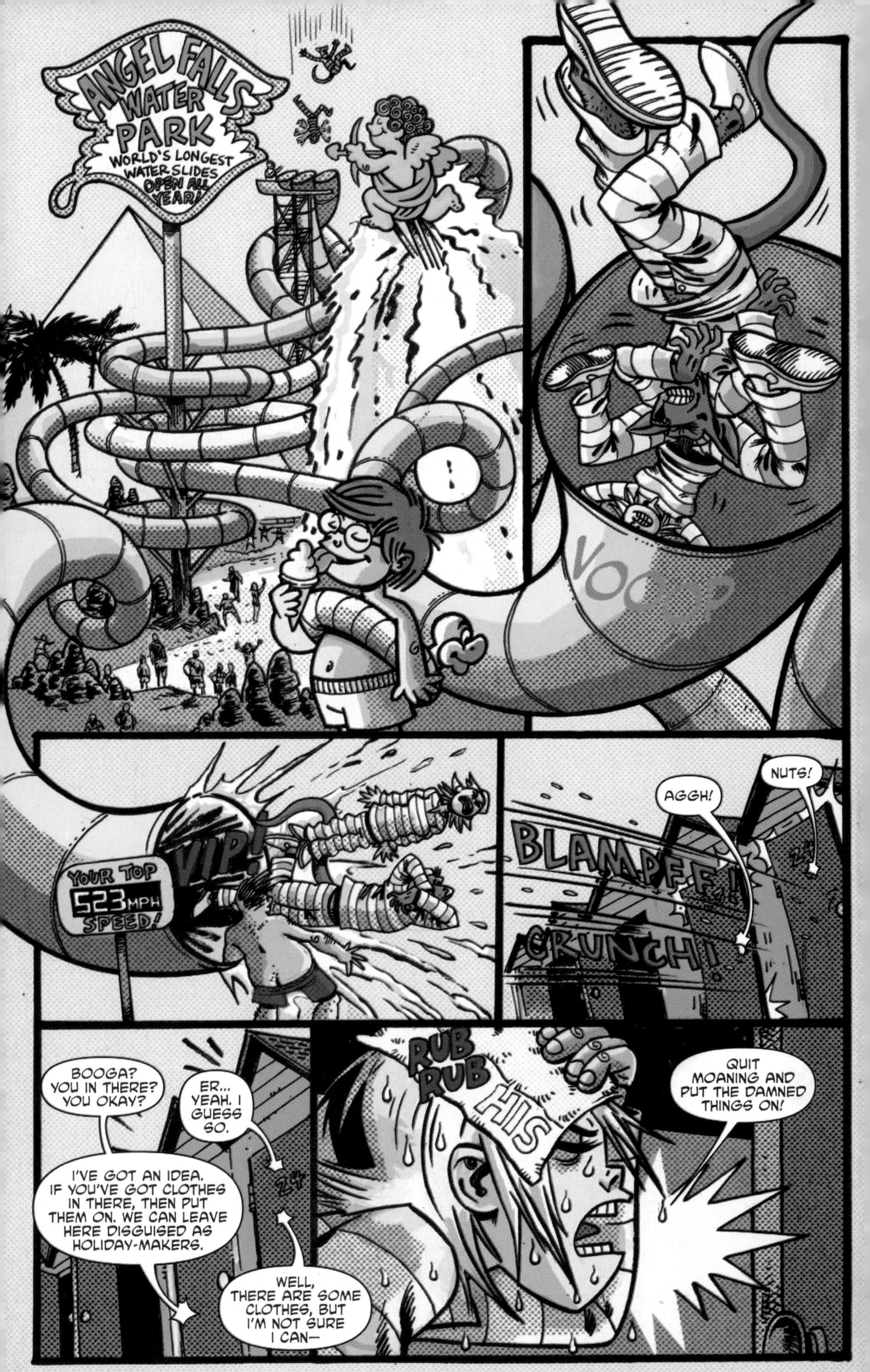
ANGEL FALLS WATER PARK
WORLD'S LONGEST WATER SLIDES OPEN ALL YEAR!
VOOOOP
YOUR TOP 523MPH SPEED!
VIP!
AGGH!
NUTS!
BLAMPFF!
CRUNCH!
BOOGA? YOU IN THERE? YOU OKAY?
ER... YEAH. I GUESS SO.
I'VE GOT AN IDEA. IF YOU'VE GOT CLOTHES IN THERE, THEN PUT THEM ON. WE CAN LEAVE HERE DISGUISED AS HOLIDAY-MAKERS.
WELL, THERE ARE SOME CLOTHES, BUT I'M NOT SURE I CAN—
RUB RUB
HIS
QUIT MOANING AND PUT THE DAMNED THINGS ON!

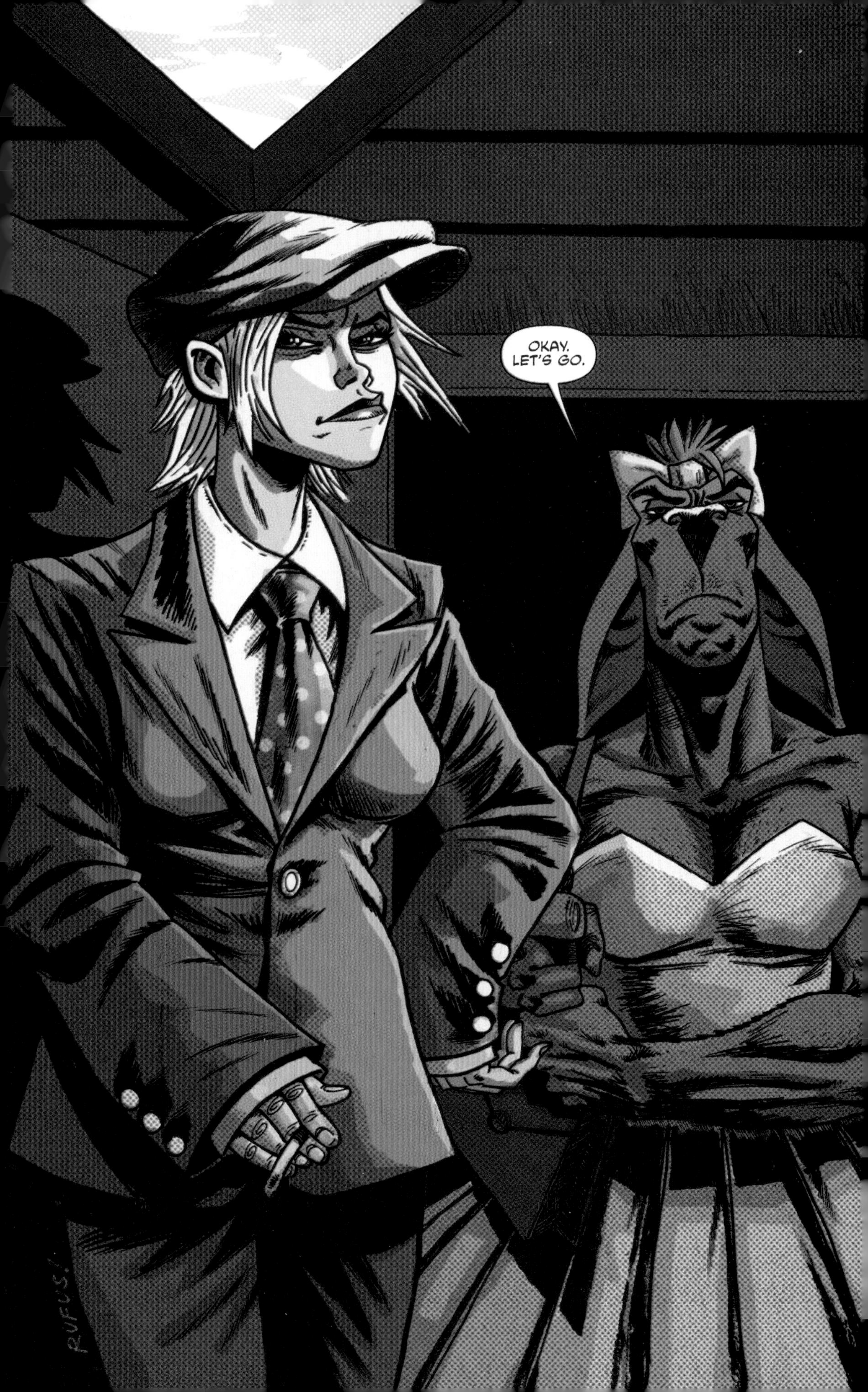
OKAY. LET'S GO.
RUFUS!

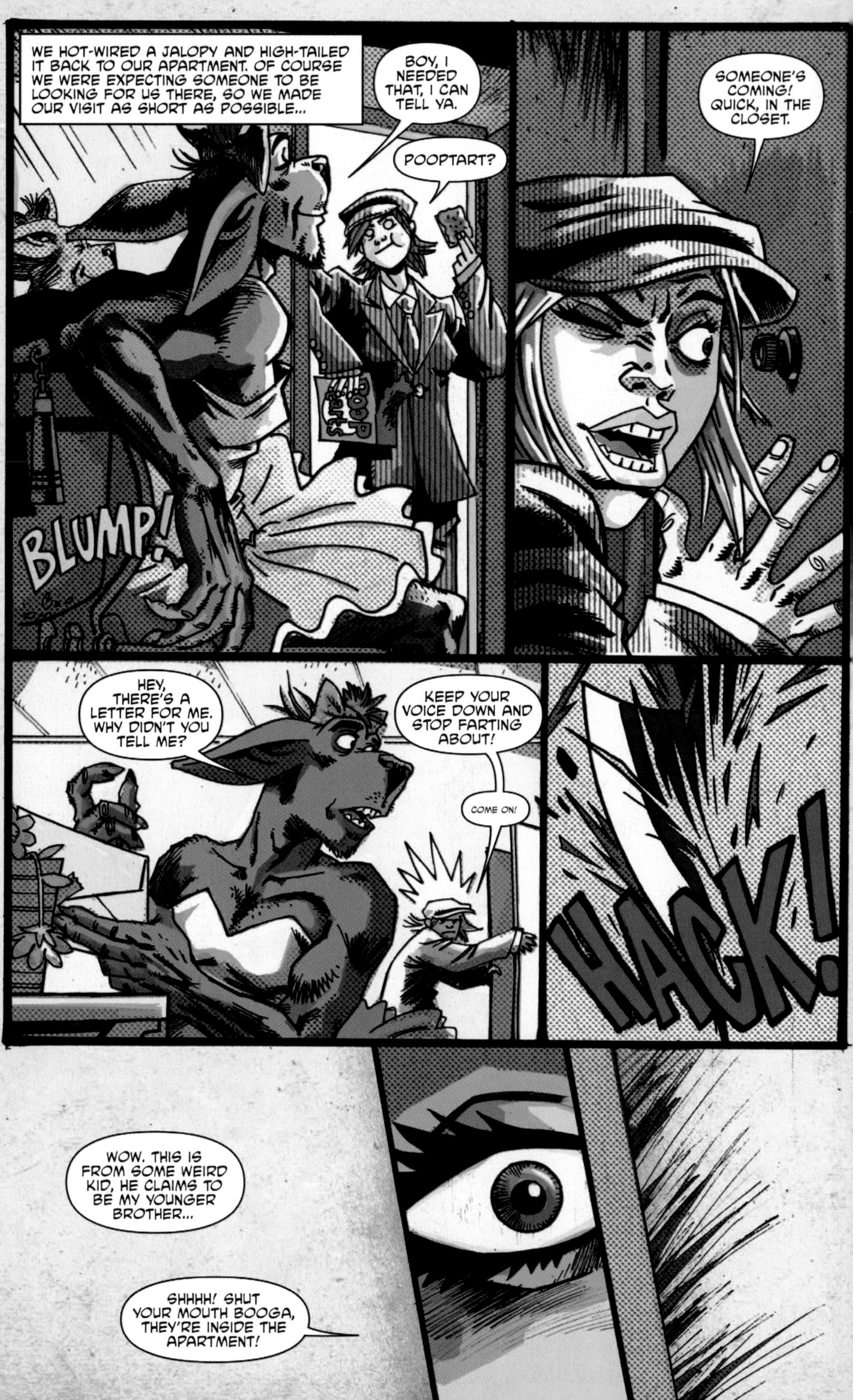

WE HOT-WIRED A JALOPY AND HIGH-TAILED IT BACK TO OUR APARTMENT. OF COURSE WE WERE EXPECTING SOMEONE TO BE LOOKING FOR US THERE, SO WE MADE OUR VISIT AS SHORT AS POSSIBLE...
BOY, I NEEDED THAT, I CAN TELL YA.
POOPTART?
BLUMP!
SOMEONE'S COMING! QUICK, IN THE CLOSET.
HEY, THERE'S A LETTER FOR ME. WHY DIDN'T YOU TELL ME?
KEEP YOUR VOICE DOWN AND STOP FARTING ABOUT!
COME ON!
HACK!
WOW. THIS IS FROM SOME WEIRD KID, HE CLAIMS TO BE MY YOUNGER BROTHER...
SHHHH! SHUT YOUR MOUTH BOOGA, THEY'RE INSIDE THE APARTMENT!

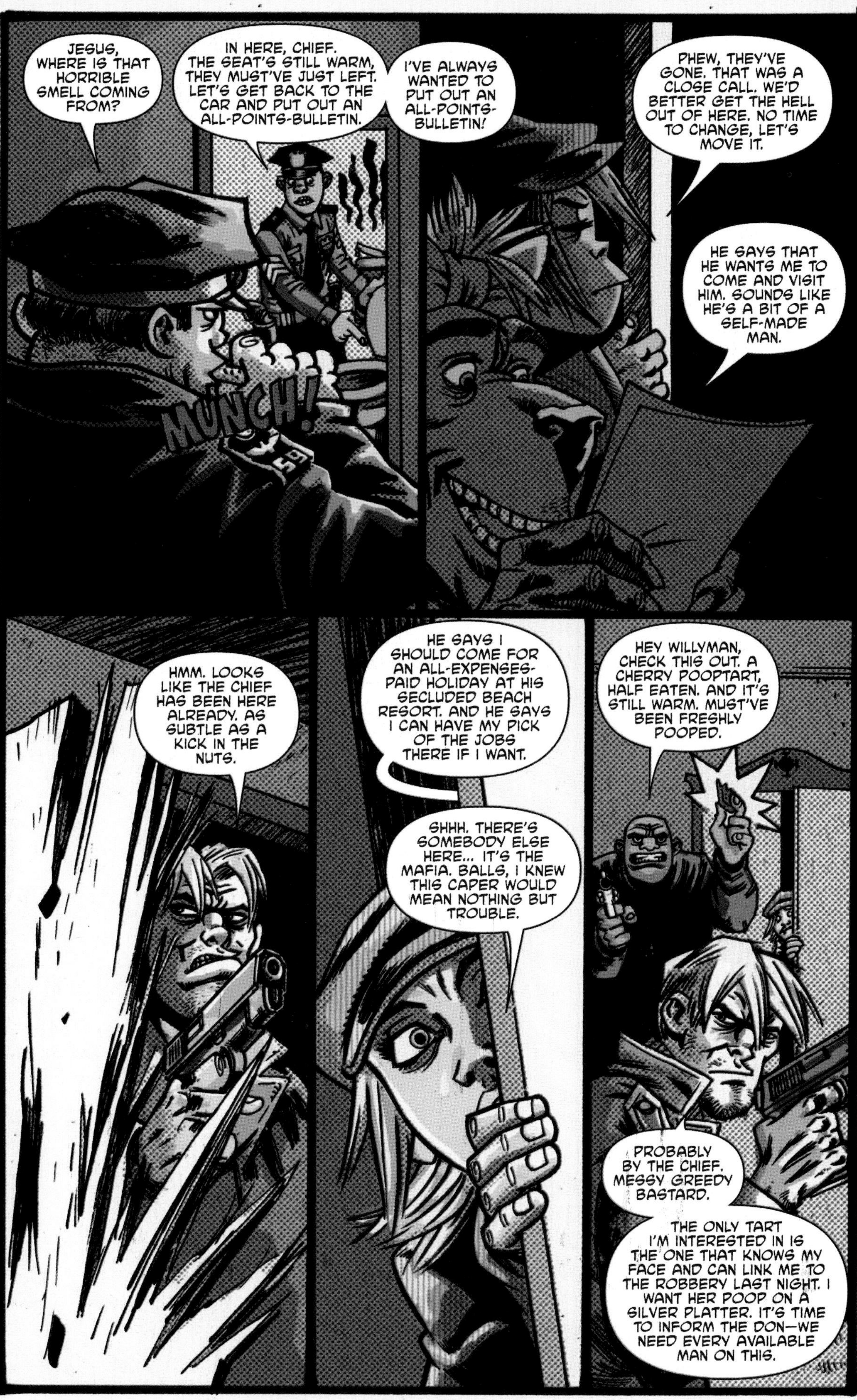
JESUS, WHERE IS THAT HORRIBLE SMELL COMING FROM?
IN HERE, CHIEF. THE SEAT'S STILL WARM, THEY MUST'VE JUST LEFT. LET'S GET BACK TO THE CAR AND PUT OUT AN ALL-POINTS-BULLETIN.
I'VE ALWAYS WANTED TO PUT OUT AN ALL-POINTS-BULLETIN!
MUNCH!
PHEW, THEY'VE GONE. THAT WAS A CLOSE CALL. WE'D BETTER GET THE HELL OUT OF HERE. NO TIME TO CHANGE, LET'S MOVE IT.
HE SAYS THAT HE WANTS ME TO COME AND VISIT HIM. SOUNDS LIKE HE'S A BIT OF A SELF-MADE MAN.
HMM. LOOKS LIKE THE CHIEF HAS BEEN HERE ALREADY. AS SUBTLE AS A KICK IN THE NUTS.
HE SAYS I SHOULD COME FOR AN ALL-EXPENSES-PAID HOLIDAY AT HIS SECLUDED BEACH RESORT. AND HE SAYS I CAN HAVE MY PICK OF THE JOBS THERE IF I WANT.
SHHH. THERE'S SOMEBODY ELSE HERE... IT'S THE MAFIA. BALLS, I KNEW THIS CAPER WOULD MEAN NOTHING BUT TROUBLE.
HEY WILLYMAN, CHECK THIS OUT. A CHERRY POOPTART, HALF EATEN. AND IT'S STILL WARM. MUST'VE BEEN FRESHLY POOPED.
PROBABLY BY THE CHIEF. MESSY GREEDY BASTARD.
THE ONLY TART I'M INTERESTED IN IS THE ONE THAT KNOWS MY FACE AND CAN LINK ME TO THE ROBBERY LAST NIGHT. I WANT HER POOP ON A SILVER PLATTER. IT'S TIME TO INFORM THE DON—WE NEED EVERY AVAILABLE MAN ON THIS.

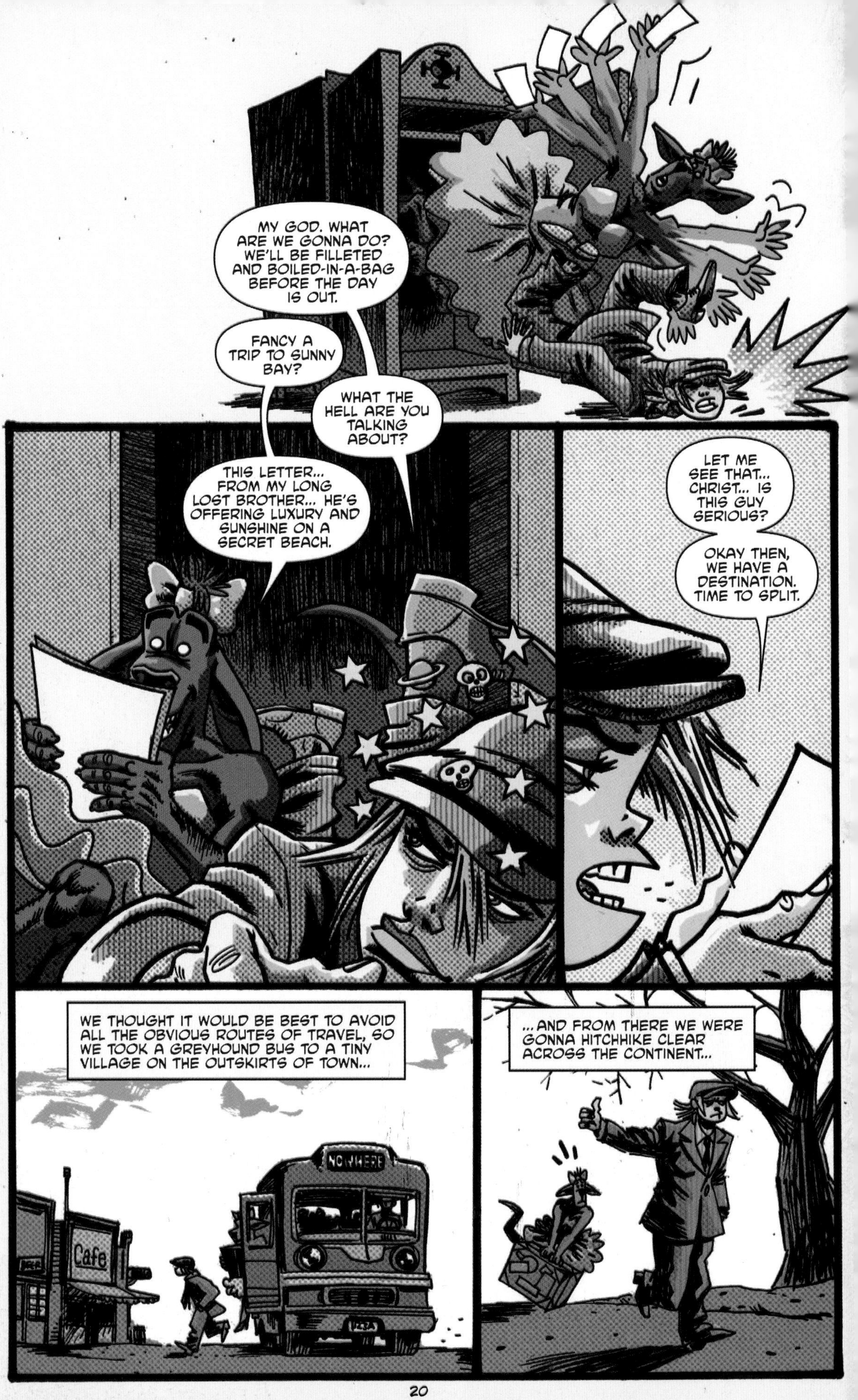
MY GOD. WHAT ARE WE GONNA DO? WE'LL BE FILLETED AND BOILED-IN-A-BAG BEFORE THE DAY IS OUT.
FANCY A TRIP TO SUNNY BAY?
WHAT THE HELL ARE YOU TALKING ABOUT?
THIS LETTER... FROM MY LONG LOST BROTHER... HE'S OFFERING LUXURY AND SUNSHINE ON A SECRET BEACH.
LET ME SEE THAT... CHRIST... IS THIS GUY SERIOUS?
OKAY THEN, WE HAVE A DESTINATION. TIME TO SPLIT.
WE THOUGHT IT WOULD BE BEST TO AVOID ALL THE OBVIOUS ROUTES OF TRAVEL, SO WE TOOK A GREYHOUND BUS TO A TINY VILLAGE ON THE OUTSKIRTS OF TOWN...
NOWHERE
Cafe
...AND FROM THERE WE WERE GONNA HITCHHIKE CLEAR ACROSS THE CONTINENT...

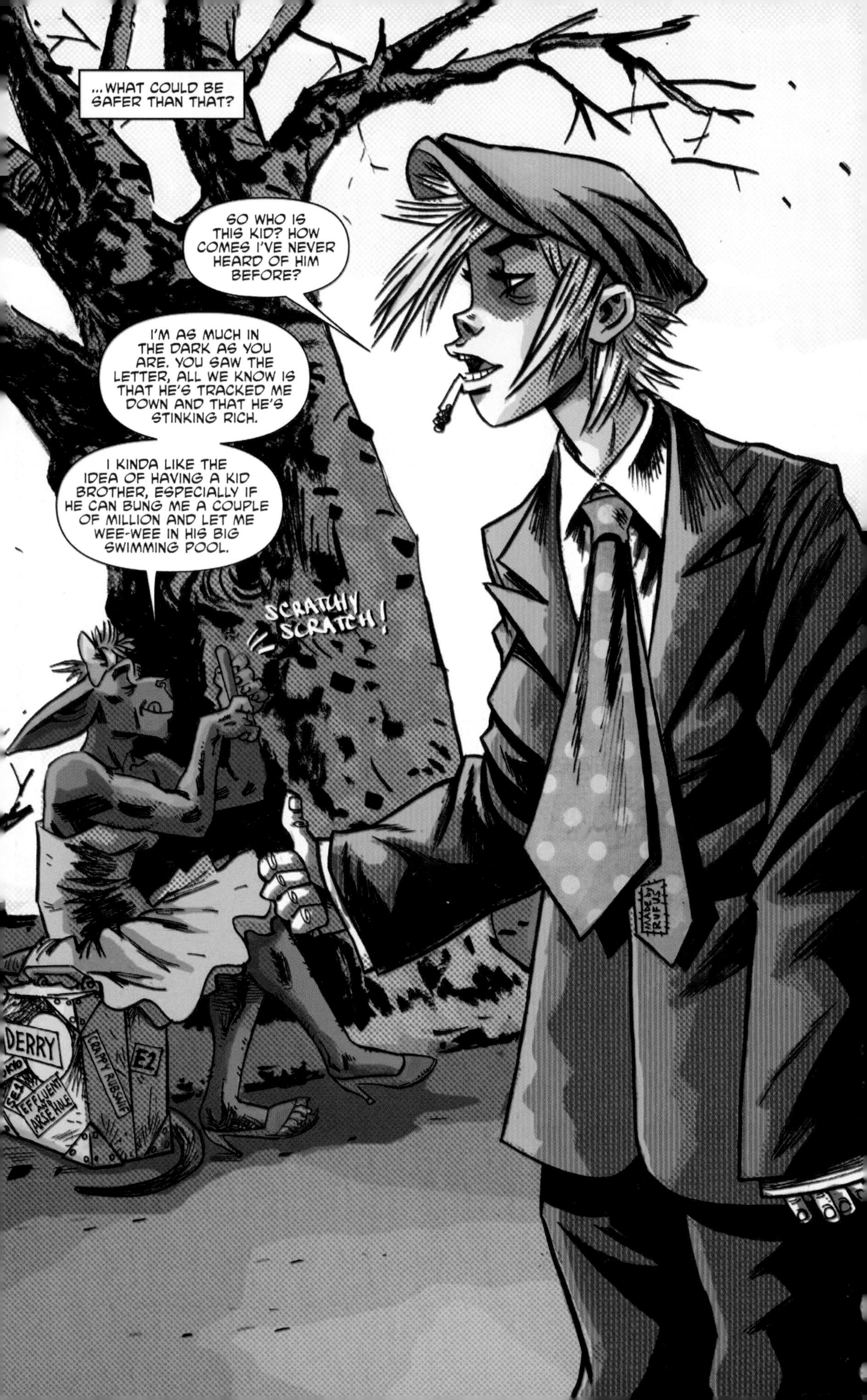
...WHAT COULD BE SAFER THAN THAT?
SO WHO IS THIS KID? HOW COMES I'VE NEVER HEARD OF HIM BEFORE?
I'M AS MUCH IN THE DARK AS YOU ARE. YOU SAW THE LETTER, ALL WE KNOW IS THAT HE'S TRACKED ME DOWN AND THAT HE'S STINKING RICH.
I KINDA LIKE THE IDEA OF HAVING A KID BROTHER, ESPECIALLY IF HE CAN BUNG ME A COUPLE OF MILLION AND LET ME WEE-WEE IN HIS BIG SWIMMING POOL.
SCRATCHY SCRATCH!
DERRY
E2
CRAPPY RUBBISH
EFFLUENT AND ARSEHOLE
SE1
MADE BY RUFUS

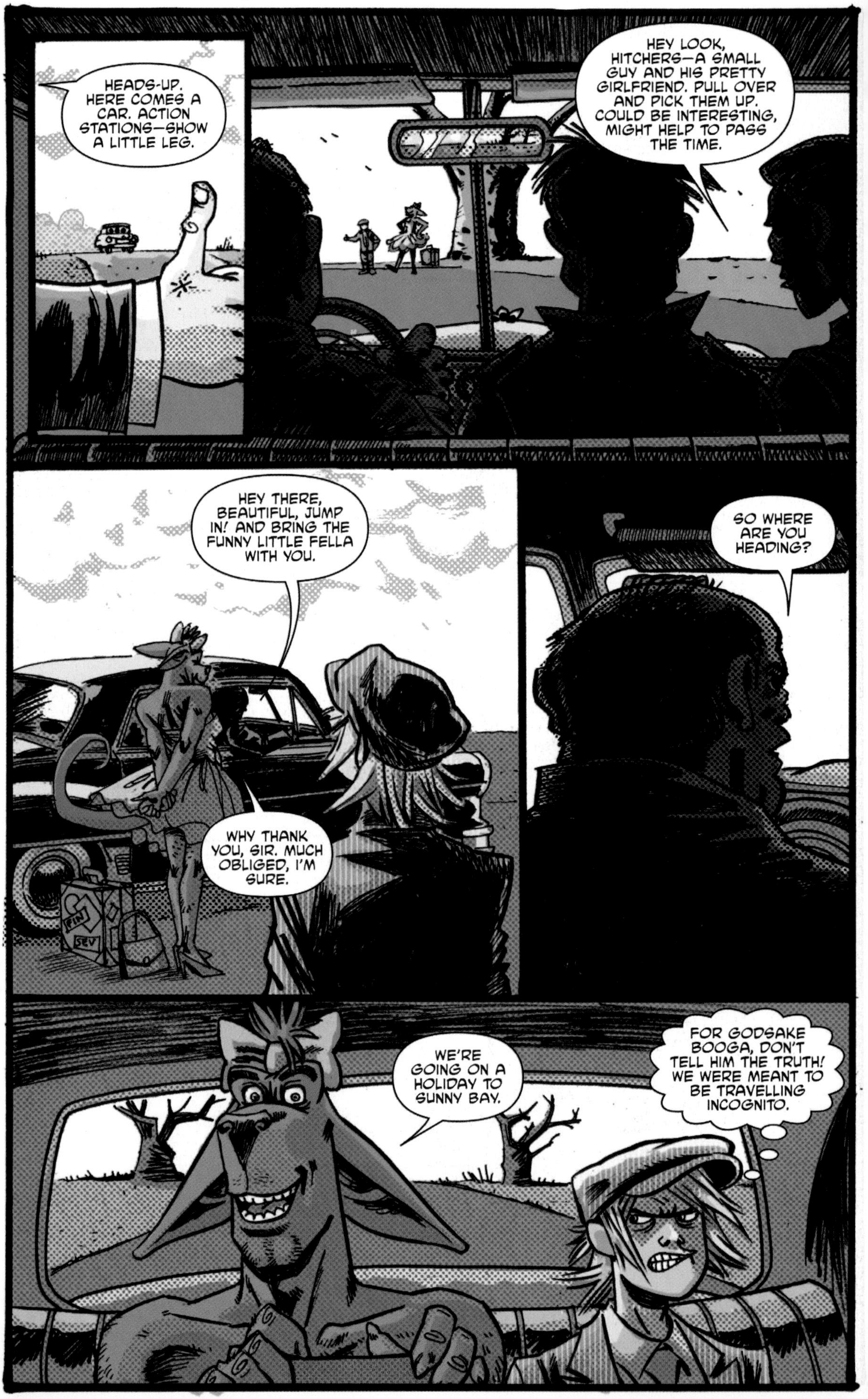
HEADS-UP. HERE COMES A CAR. ACTION STATIONS—SHOW A LITTLE LEG.
HEY LOOK, HITCHERS—A SMALL GUY AND HIS PRETTY GIRLFRIEND. PULL OVER AND PICK THEM UP. COULD BE INTERESTING, MIGHT HELP TO PASS THE TIME.
HEY THERE, BEAUTIFUL, JUMP IN! AND BRING THE FUNNY LITTLE FELLA WITH YOU.
WHY THANK YOU, SIR. MUCH OBLIGED, I'M SURE.
FIN
SEV
SO WHERE ARE YOU HEADING?
WE'RE GOING ON A HOLIDAY TO SUNNY BAY.
FOR GODSAKE BOOGA, DON'T TELL HIM THE TRUTH! WE WERE MEANT TO BE TRAVELLING INCOGNITO.

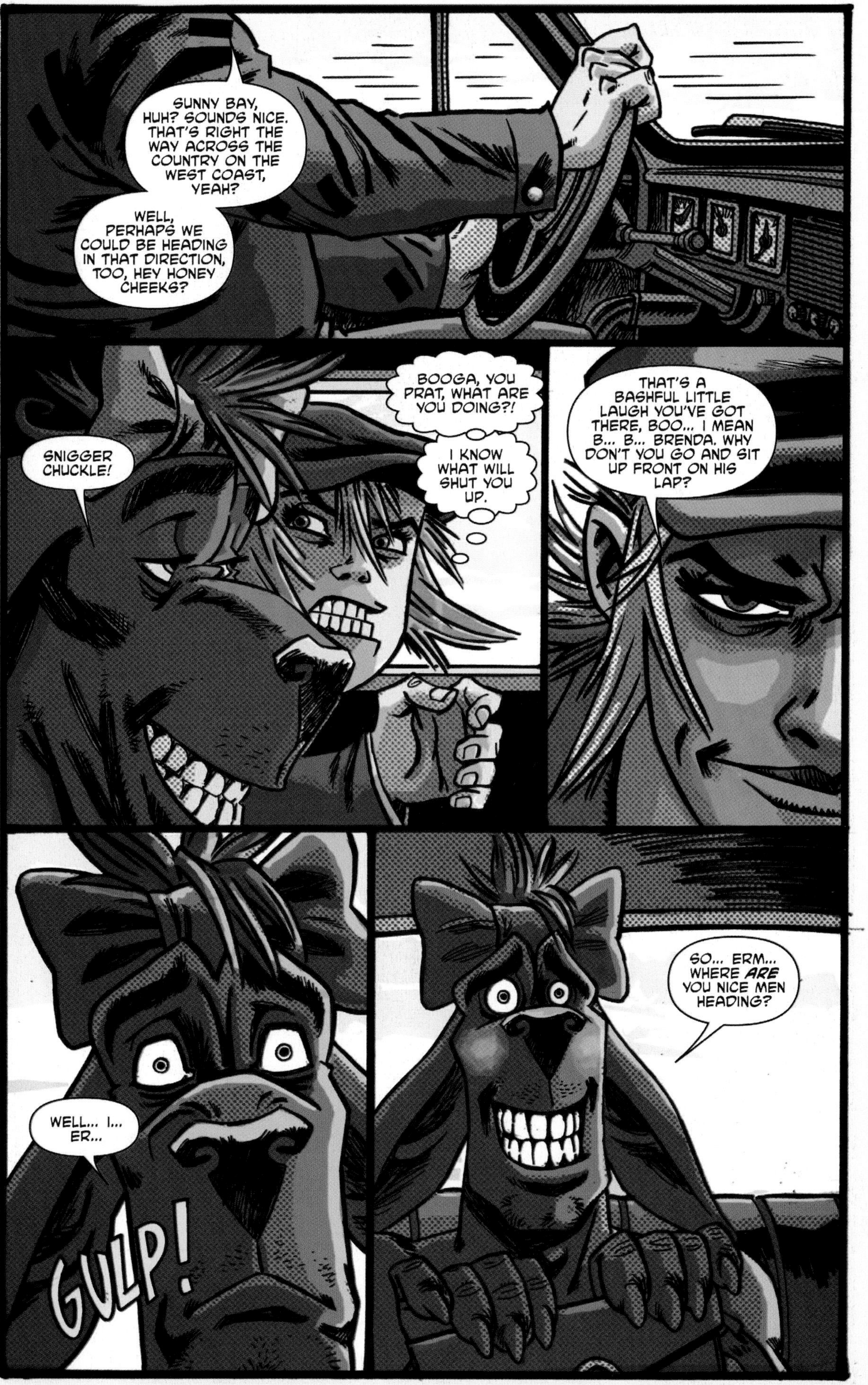
SUNNY BAY, HUH? SOUNDS NICE. THAT'S RIGHT THE WAY ACROSS THE COUNTRY ON THE WEST COAST, YEAH?
WELL, PERHAPS WE COULD BE HEADING IN THAT DIRECTION, TOO, HEY HONEY CHEEKS?
SNIGGER CHUCKLE!
BOOGA, YOU PRAT, WHAT ARE YOU DOING?!
I KNOW WHAT WILL SHUT YOU UP.
THAT'S A BASHFUL LITTLE LAUGH YOU'VE GOT THERE, BOO... I MEAN B... B... BRENDA. WHY DON'T YOU GO AND SIT UP FRONT ON HIS LAP?
WELL... I... ER...
GULP!
SO... ERM... WHERE *ARE* YOU NICE MEN HEADING?

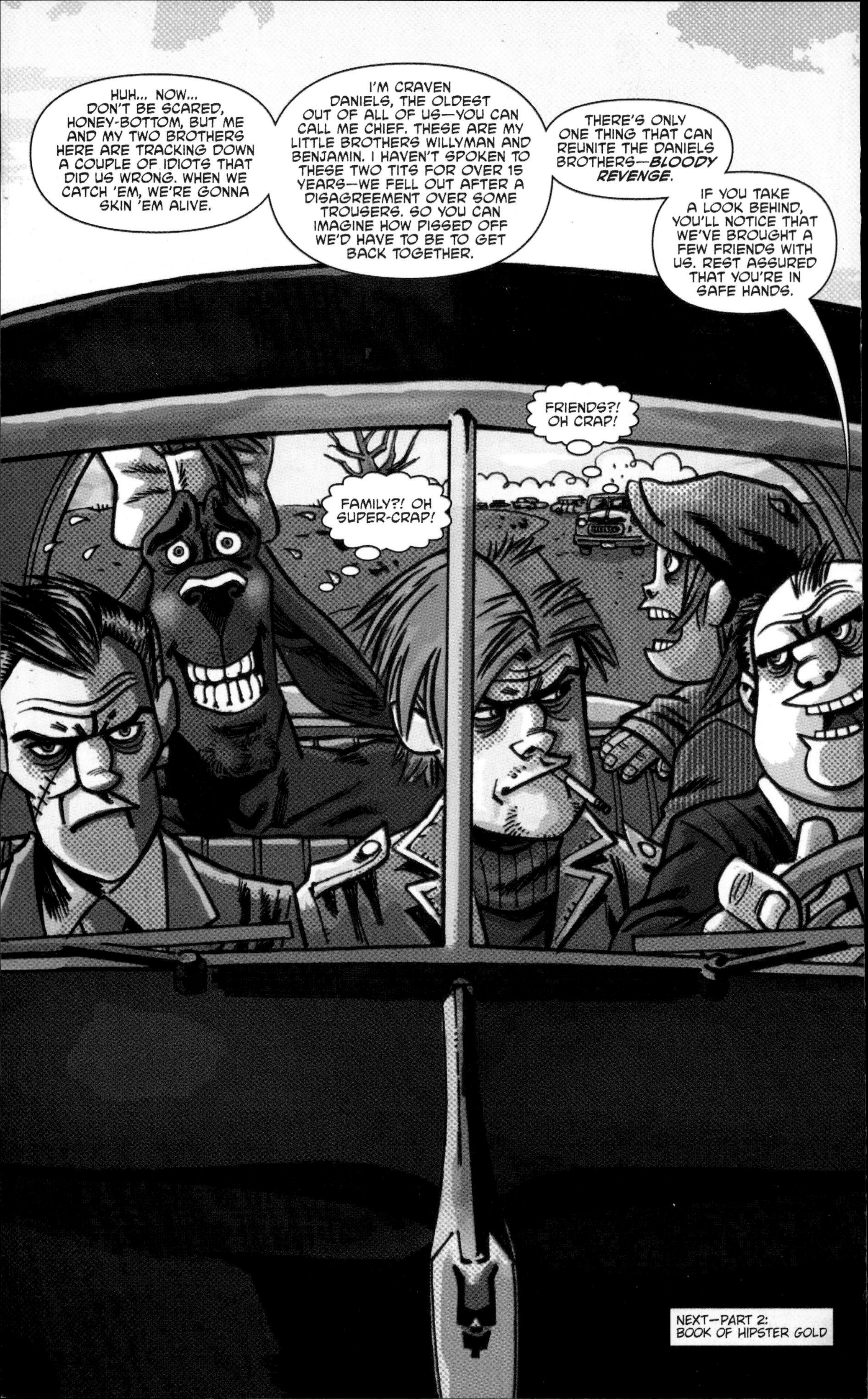
HUH... NOW... DON'T BE SCARED, HONEY-BOTTOM, BUT ME AND MY TWO BROTHERS HERE ARE TRACKING DOWN A COUPLE OF IDIOTS THAT DID US WRONG. WHEN WE CATCH 'EM, WE'RE GONNA SKIN 'EM ALIVE.
I'M CRAVEN DANIELS, THE OLDEST OUT OF ALL OF US—YOU CAN CALL ME CHIEF. THESE ARE MY LITTLE BROTHERS WILLYMAN AND BENJAMIN. I HAVEN'T SPOKEN TO THESE TWO TITS FOR OVER 15 YEARS—WE FELL OUT AFTER A DISAGREEMENT OVER SOME TROUSERS. SO YOU CAN IMAGINE HOW PISSED OFF WE'D HAVE TO BE TO GET BACK TOGETHER.
THERE'S ONLY ONE THING THAT CAN REUNITE THE DANIELS BROTHERS—*BLOODY REVENGE*.
IF YOU TAKE A LOOK BEHIND, YOU'LL NOTICE THAT WE'VE BROUGHT A FEW FRIENDS WITH US. REST ASSURED THAT YOU'RE IN SAFE HANDS.
FRIENDS?! OH CRAP!
FAMILY?! OH SUPER-CRAP!
NEXT—PART 2: BOOK OF HIPSTER GOLD

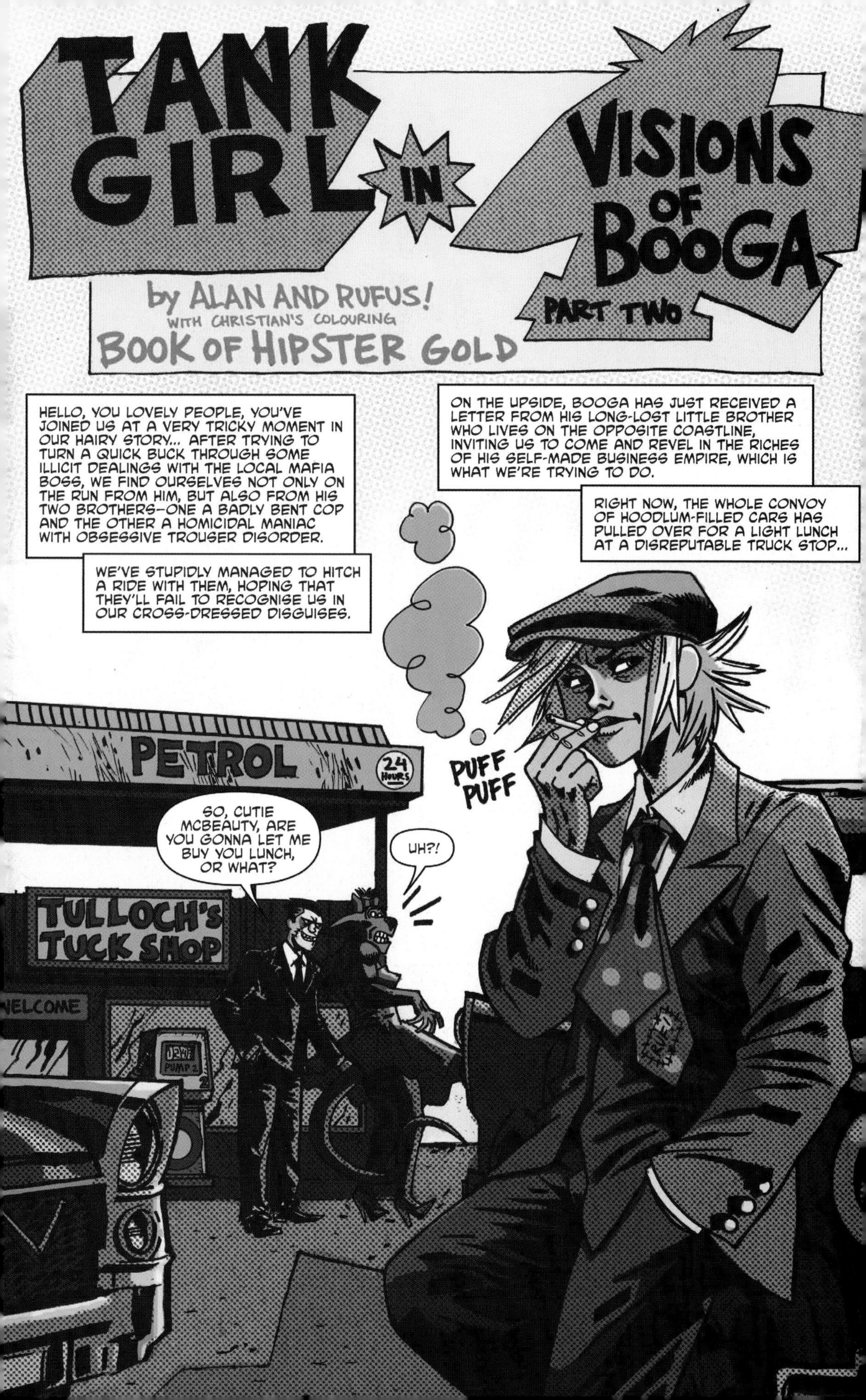
TANK GIRL IN VISIONS OF BOOGA
PART TWO
by ALAN AND RUFUS!
WITH CHRISTIAN'S COLOURING
BOOK OF HIPSTER GOLD
HELLO, YOU LOVELY PEOPLE, YOU'VE JOINED US AT A VERY TRICKY MOMENT IN OUR HAIRY STORY... AFTER TRYING TO TURN A QUICK BUCK THROUGH SOME ILLICIT DEALINGS WITH THE LOCAL MAFIA BOSS, WE FIND OURSELVES NOT ONLY ON THE RUN FROM HIM, BUT ALSO FROM HIS TWO BROTHERS–ONE A BADLY BENT COP AND THE OTHER A HOMICIDAL MANIAC WITH OBSESSIVE TROUSER DISORDER.
WE'VE STUPIDLY MANAGED TO HITCH A RIDE WITH THEM, HOPING THAT THEY'LL FAIL TO RECOGNISE US IN OUR CROSS-DRESSED DISGUISES.
ON THE UPSIDE, BOOGA HAS JUST RECEIVED A LETTER FROM HIS LONG-LOST LITTLE BROTHER WHO LIVES ON THE OPPOSITE COASTLINE, INVITING US TO COME AND REVEL IN THE RICHES OF HIS SELF-MADE BUSINESS EMPIRE, WHICH IS WHAT WE'RE TRYING TO DO.
RIGHT NOW, THE WHOLE CONVOY OF HOODLUM-FILLED CARS HAS PULLED OVER FOR A LIGHT LUNCH AT A DISREPUTABLE TRUCK STOP...
PETROL
24 HOURS
PUFF PUFF
SO, CUTIE MCBEAUTY, ARE YOU GONNA LET ME BUY YOU LUNCH, OR WHAT?
UH?!
TULLOCH'S TUCK SHOP
WELCOME
PUMP 2

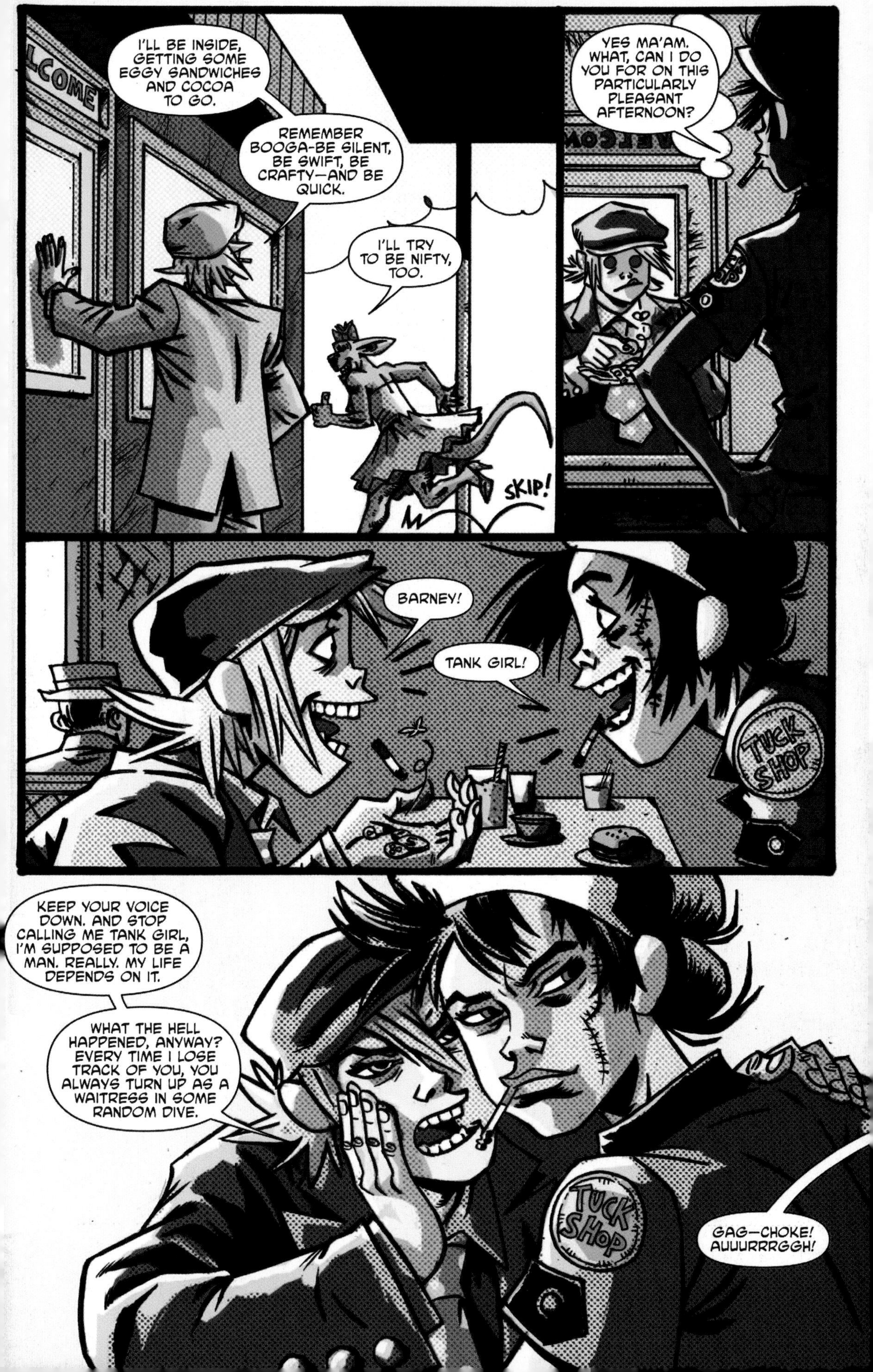

I'LL BE INSIDE, GETTING SOME EGGY SANDWICHES AND COCOA TO GO.
REMEMBER BOOGA-BE SILENT, BE SWIFT, BE CRAFTY—AND BE QUICK.
I'LL TRY TO BE NIFTY, TOO.
SKIP!
YES MA'AM. WHAT, CAN I DO YOU FOR ON THIS PARTICULARLY PLEASANT AFTERNOON?
BARNEY!
TANK GIRL!
TUCK SHOP
KEEP YOUR VOICE DOWN. AND STOP CALLING ME TANK GIRL, I'M SUPPOSED TO BE A MAN. REALLY. MY LIFE DEPENDS ON IT.
WHAT THE HELL HAPPENED, ANYWAY? EVERY TIME I LOSE TRACK OF YOU, YOU ALWAYS TURN UP AS A WAITRESS IN SOME RANDOM DIVE.
TUCK SHOP
GAG—CHOKE! AUUURRRGGH!

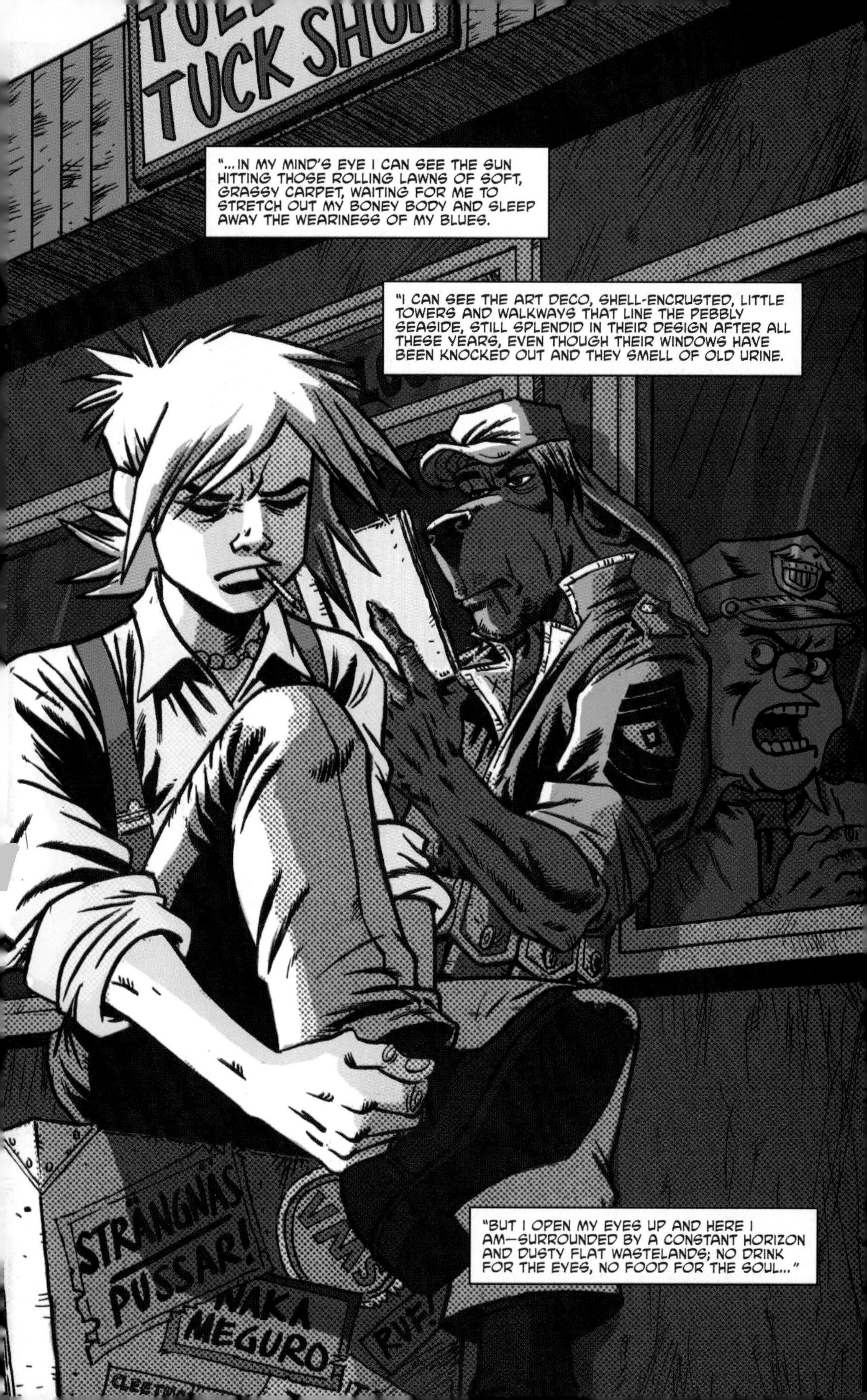
"...IN MY MIND'S EYE I CAN SEE THE SUN HITTING THOSE ROLLING LAWNS OF SOFT, GRASSY CARPET, WAITING FOR ME TO STRETCH OUT MY BONEY BODY AND SLEEP AWAY THE WEARINESS OF MY BLUES.
"I CAN SEE THE ART DECO, SHELL-ENCRUSTED, LITTLE TOWERS AND WALKWAYS THAT LINE THE PEBBLY SEASIDE, STILL SPLENDID IN THEIR DESIGN AFTER ALL THESE YEARS, EVEN THOUGH THEIR WINDOWS HAVE BEEN KNOCKED OUT AND THEY SMELL OF OLD URINE.
"BUT I OPEN MY EYES UP AND HERE I AM—SURROUNDED BY A CONSTANT HORIZON AND DUSTY FLAT WASTELANDS; NO DRINK FOR THE EYES, NO FOOD FOR THE SOUL..."
STRÄNGNÄS PUSSAR!
NAKA MEGURO

WE ARE THE DESPERATE DAN APPRECIATION SOCIETY...
GOD SAVE STRAWBERRY JAM, AND ALL THE DIFFERENT VARIETIES!

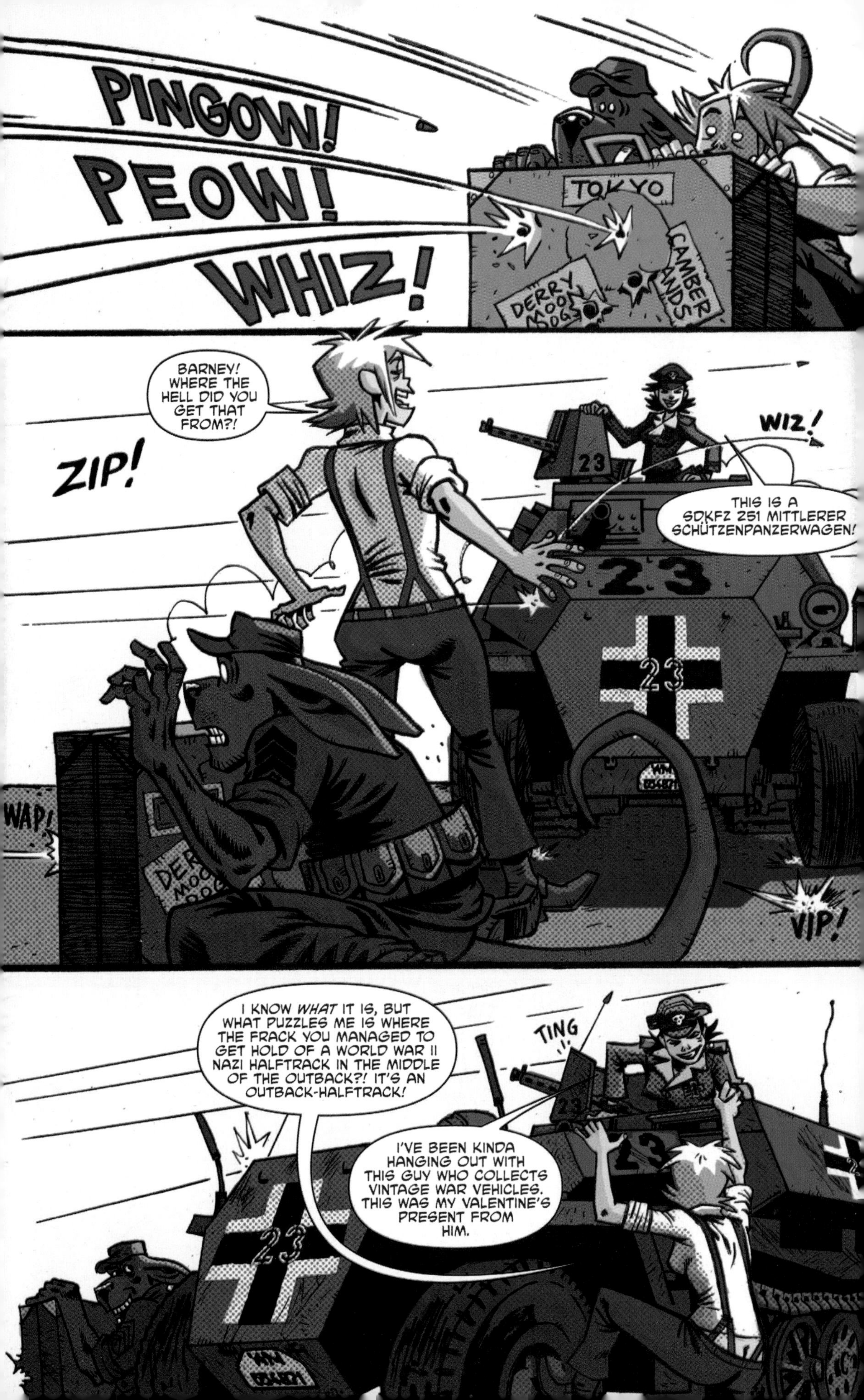
PINGOW!
PEOW!
WHIZ!
TOKYO
CAMBER SANDS
DERRY MOON DOGS
BARNEY! WHERE THE HELL DID YOU GET THAT FROM?!
ZIP!
WIZ!
THIS IS A SDKFZ 251 MITTLERER SCHÜTZENPANZERWAGEN!
23
WAP!
VIP!
I KNOW *WHAT* IT IS, BUT WHAT PUZZLES ME IS WHERE THE FRACK YOU MANAGED TO GET HOLD OF A WORLD WAR II NAZI HALFTRACK IN THE MIDDLE OF THE OUTBACK?! IT'S AN OUTBACK-HALFTRACK!
TING
I'VE BEEN KINDA HANGING OUT WITH THIS GUY WHO COLLECTS VINTAGE WAR VEHICLES. THIS WAS MY VALENTINE'S PRESENT FROM HIM.

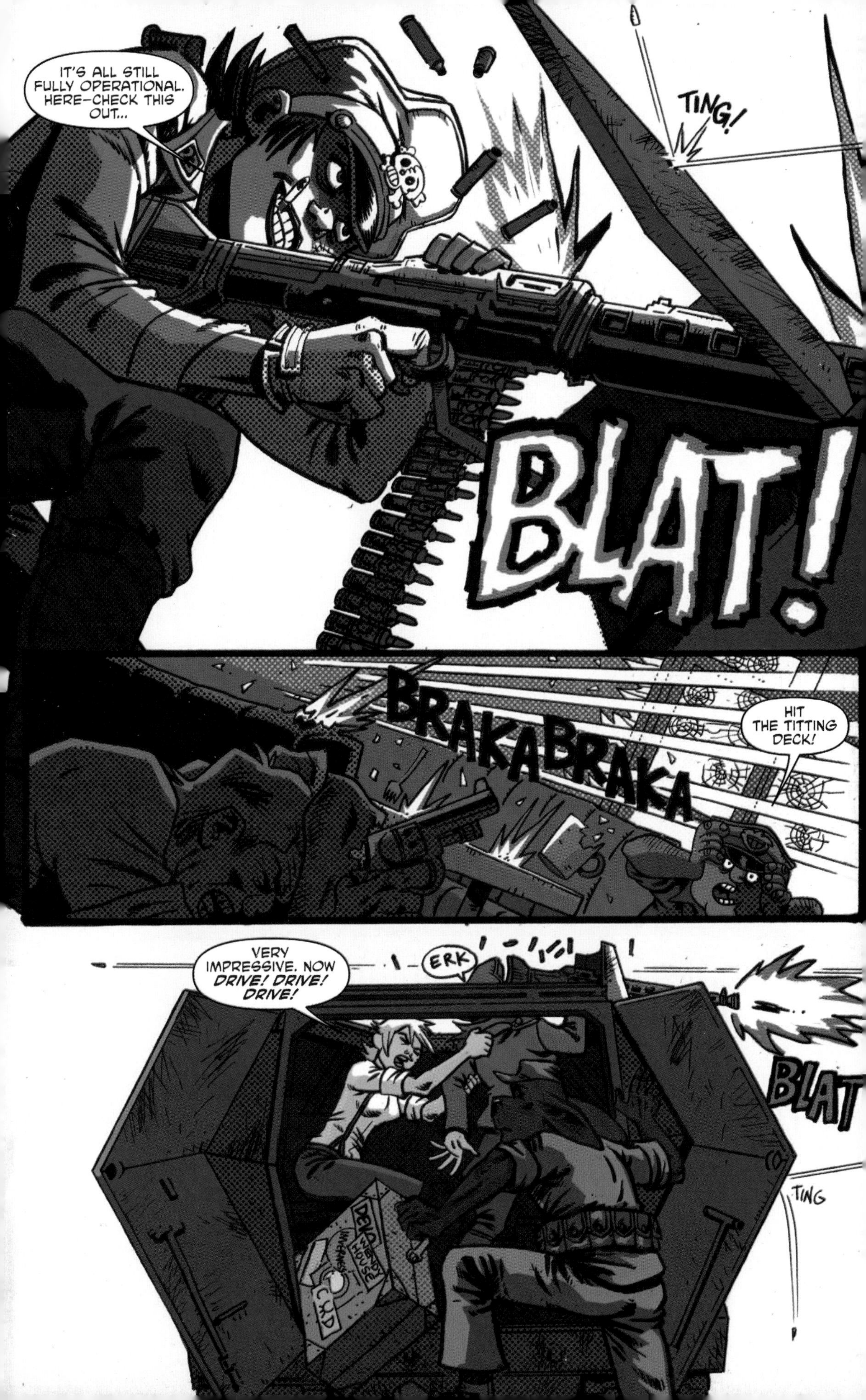
IT'S ALL STILL FULLY OPERATIONAL. HERE—CHECK THIS OUT...
TING!
BLAT!
BRAKABRAKA
HIT THE TITTING DECK!
VERY IMPRESSIVE. NOW DRIVE! DRIVE! DRIVE!
ERK
BLAT
TING

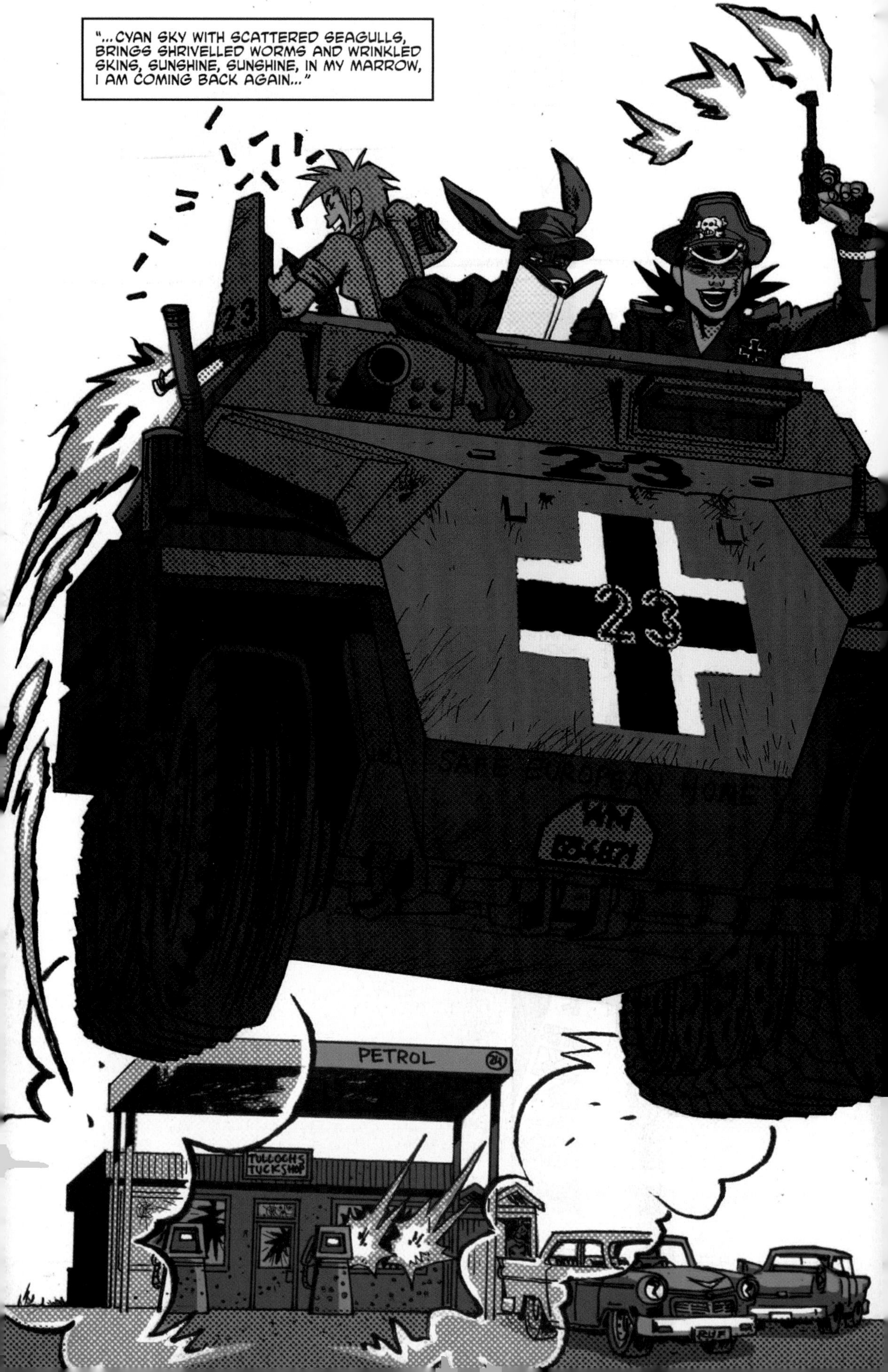
"...CYAN SKY WITH SCATTERED SEAGULLS, BRINGS SHRIVELLED WORMS AND WRINKLED SKINS, SUNSHINE, SUNSHINE, IN MY MARROW, I AM COMING BACK AGAIN..."
23
2-3
23
PETROL
TULLOCHS TUCKSHOP

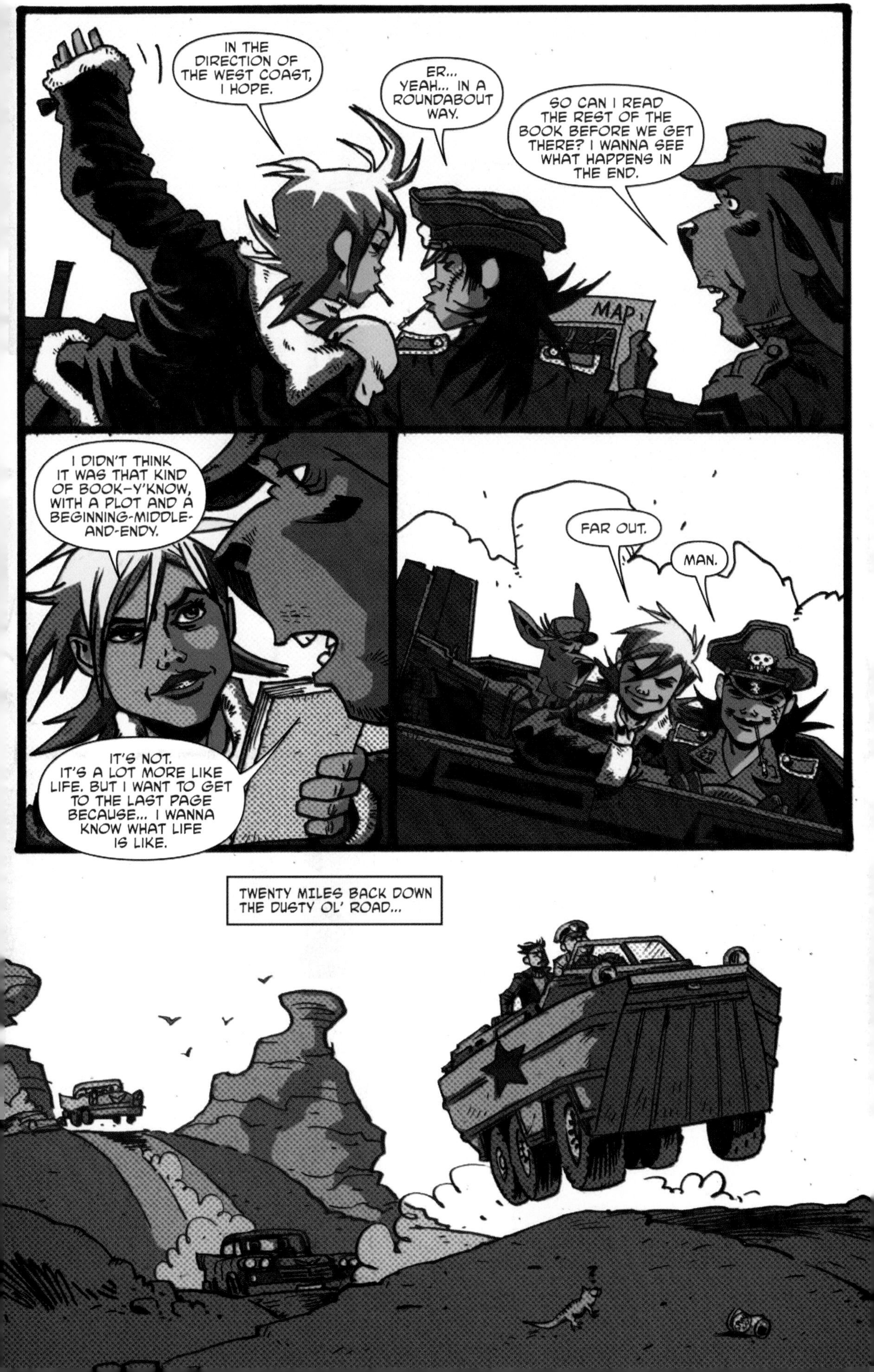
IN THE DIRECTION OF THE WEST COAST, I HOPE.
ER... YEAH... IN A ROUNDABOUT WAY.
SO CAN I READ THE REST OF THE BOOK BEFORE WE GET THERE? I WANNA SEE WHAT HAPPENS IN THE END.
MAP
I DIDN'T THINK IT WAS THAT KIND OF BOOK—Y'KNOW, WITH A PLOT AND A BEGINNING-MIDDLE-AND-ENDY.
IT'S NOT. IT'S A LOT MORE LIKE LIFE. BUT I WANT TO GET TO THE LAST PAGE BECAUSE... I WANNA KNOW WHAT LIFE IS LIKE.
FAR OUT.
MAN.
TWENTY MILES BACK DOWN THE DUSTY OL' ROAD...

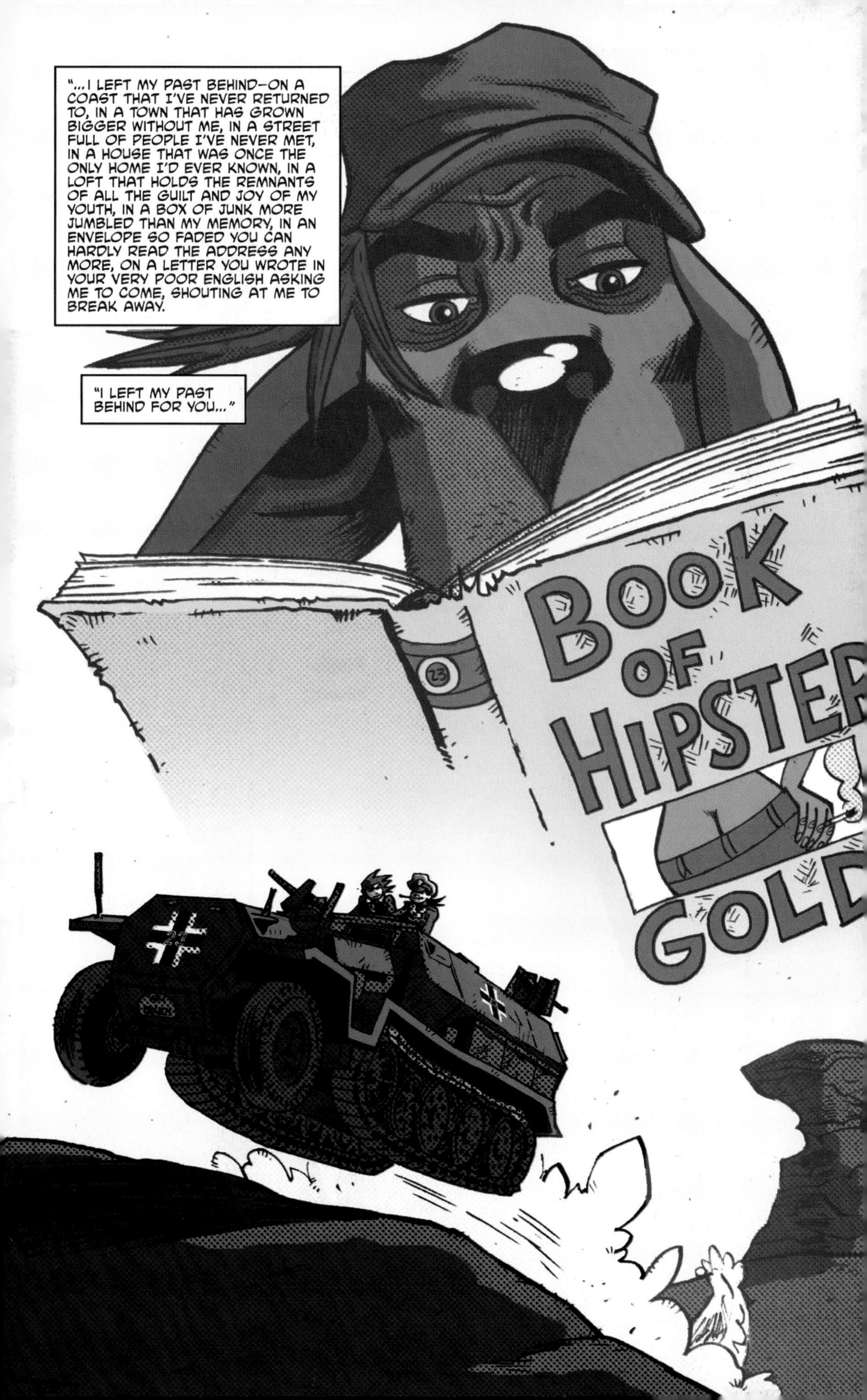
"...I LEFT MY PAST BEHIND—ON A COAST THAT I'VE NEVER RETURNED TO, IN A TOWN THAT HAS GROWN BIGGER WITHOUT ME, IN A STREET FULL OF PEOPLE I'VE NEVER MET, IN A HOUSE THAT WAS ONCE THE ONLY HOME I'D EVER KNOWN, IN A LOFT THAT HOLDS THE REMNANTS OF ALL THE GUILT AND JOY OF MY YOUTH, IN A BOX OF JUNK MORE JUMBLED THAN MY MEMORY, IN AN ENVELOPE SO FADED YOU CAN HARDLY READ THE ADDRESS ANY MORE, ON A LETTER YOU WROTE IN YOUR VERY POOR ENGLISH ASKING ME TO COME, SHOUTING AT ME TO BREAK AWAY.
"I LEFT MY PAST BEHIND FOR YOU..."
BOOK OF HIPSTER GOLD
23

NEXT: PART THREE
LETTERS TO EARTH

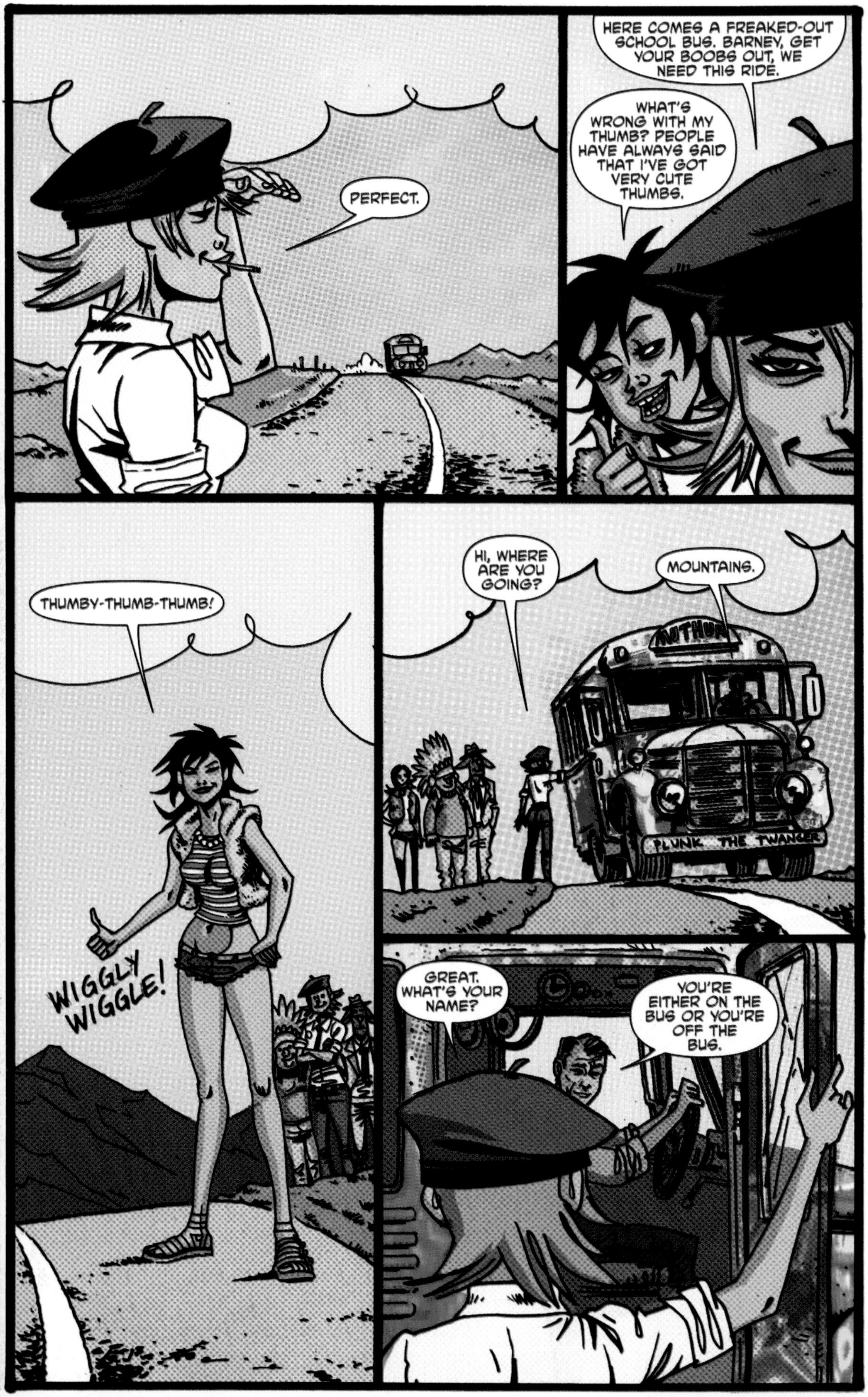
PERFECT.
HERE COMES A FREAKED-OUT SCHOOL BUS. BARNEY, GET YOUR BOOBS OUT, WE NEED THIS RIDE.
WHAT'S WRONG WITH MY THUMB? PEOPLE HAVE ALWAYS SAID THAT I'VE GOT VERY CUTE THUMBS.
THUMBY-THUMB-THUMB!
WIGGLY WIGGLE!
HI, WHERE ARE YOU GOING?
MOUNTAINS.
PLUNK THE TWANGER
GREAT. WHAT'S YOUR NAME?
YOU'RE EITHER ON THE BUS OR YOU'RE OFF THE BUS.

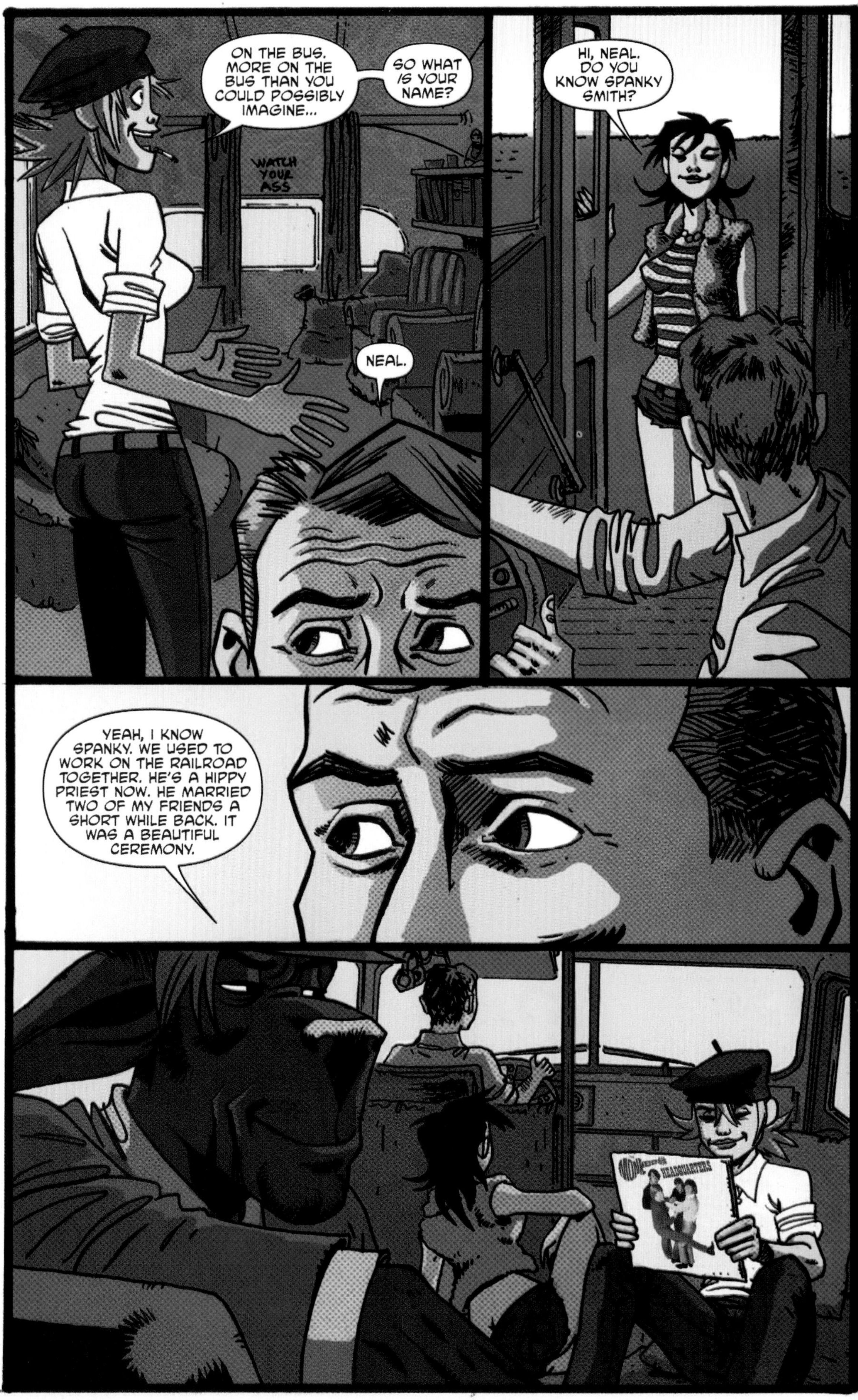
ON THE BUS. MORE ON THE BUS THAN YOU COULD POSSIBLY IMAGINE...
SO WHAT IS YOUR NAME?
WATCH YOUR ASS
NEAL.
HI, NEAL. DO YOU KNOW SPANKY SMITH?
YEAH, I KNOW SPANKY. WE USED TO WORK ON THE RAILROAD TOGETHER. HE'S A HIPPY PRIEST NOW. HE MARRIED TWO OF MY FRIENDS A SHORT WHILE BACK. IT WAS A BEAUTIFUL CEREMONY.

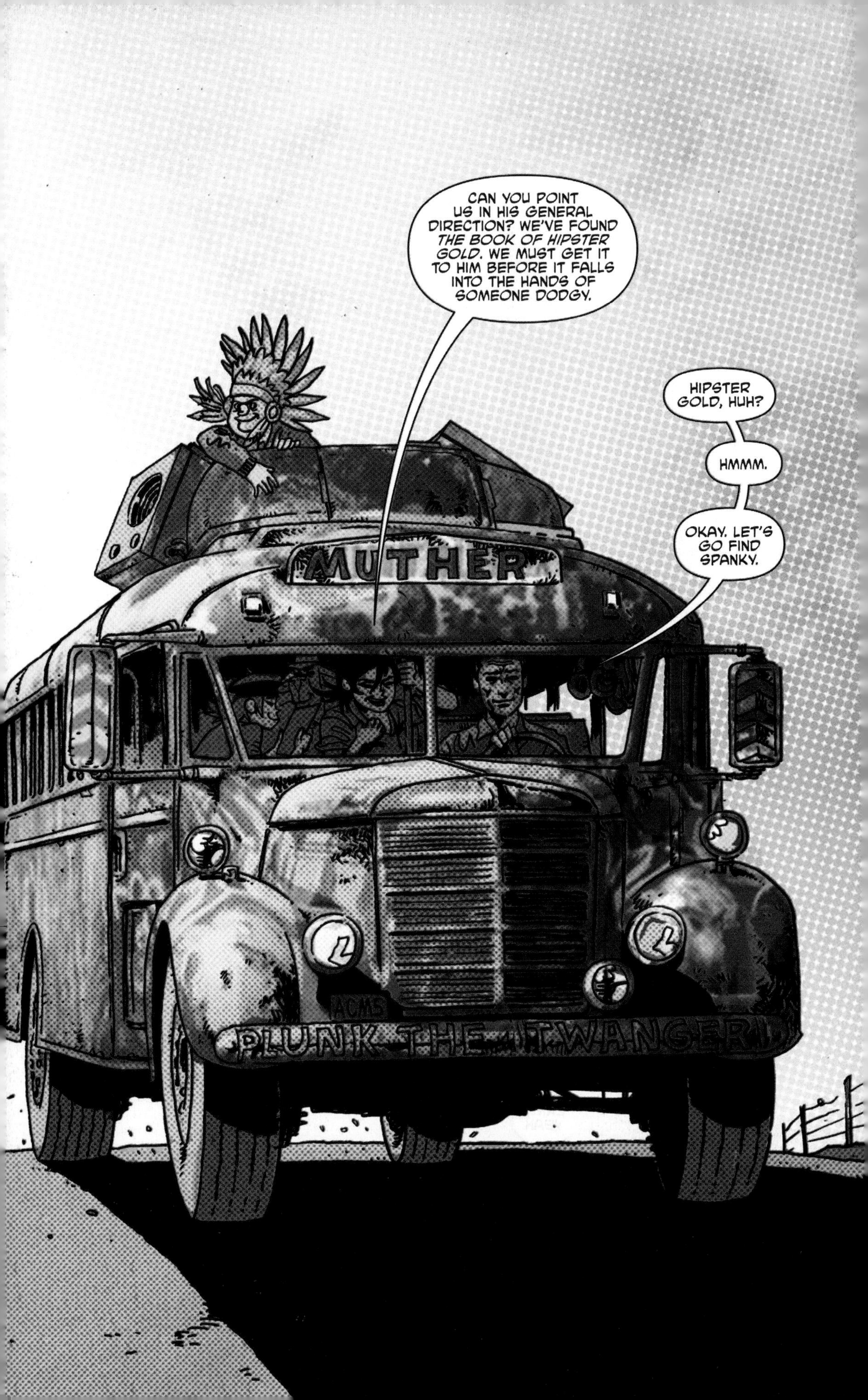
CAN YOU POINT US IN HIS GENERAL DIRECTION? WE'VE FOUND *THE BOOK OF HIPSTER GOLD*. WE MUST GET IT TO HIM BEFORE IT FALLS INTO THE HANDS OF SOMEONE DODGY.
HIPSTER GOLD, HUH?
HMMM.
OKAY. LET'S GO FIND SPANKY.
MUTHER
PLUNK THE TWANGER!

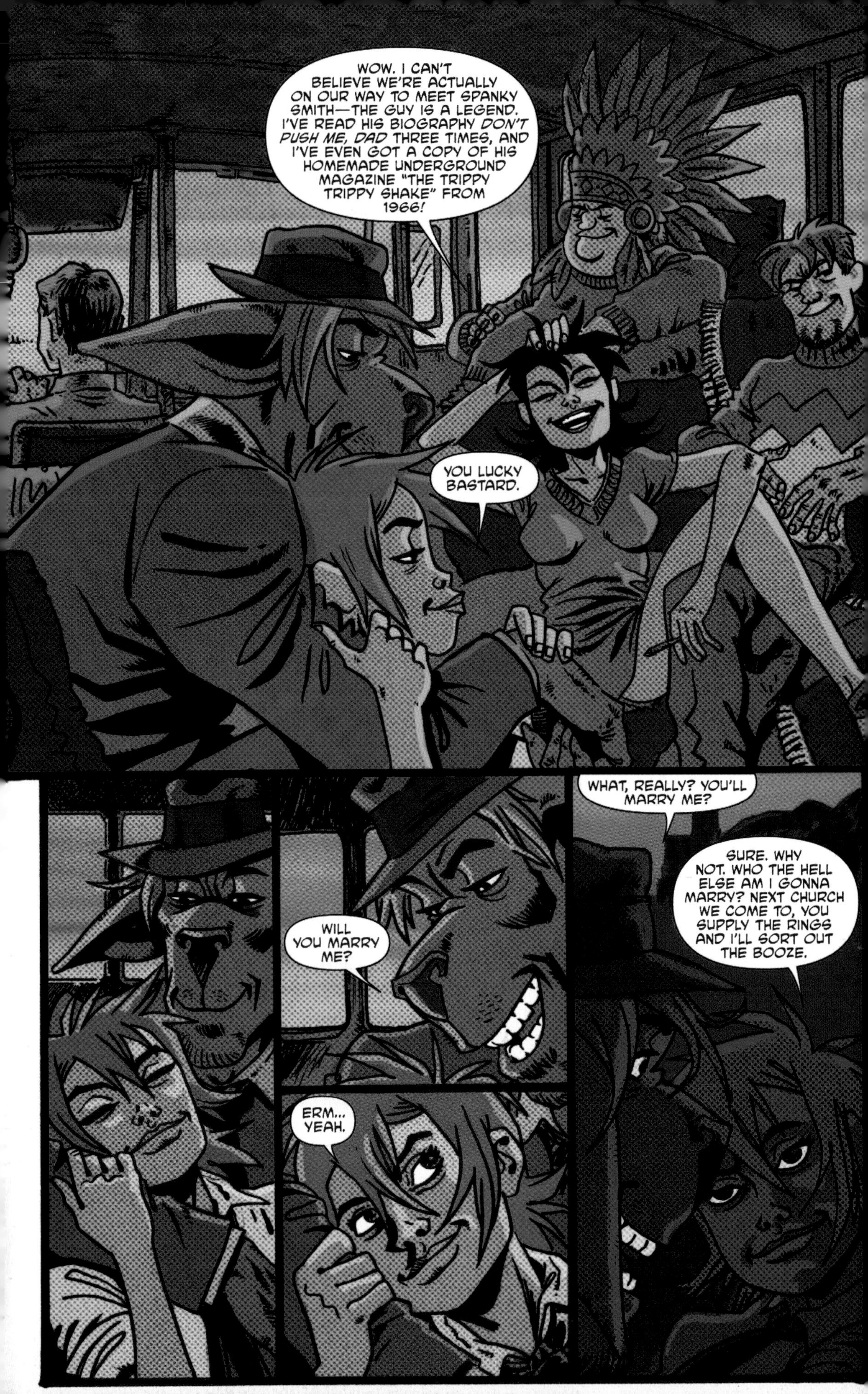
WOW. I CAN'T BELIEVE WE'RE ACTUALLY ON OUR WAY TO MEET SPANKY SMITH—THE GUY IS A LEGEND. I'VE READ HIS BIOGRAPHY *DON'T PUSH ME, DAD* THREE TIMES, AND I'VE EVEN GOT A COPY OF HIS HOMEMADE UNDERGROUND MAGAZINE "THE TRIPPY TRIPPY SHAKE" FROM *1966!*
YOU LUCKY BASTARD.
WILL YOU MARRY ME?
ERM... YEAH.
WHAT, REALLY? YOU'LL MARRY ME?
SURE. WHY NOT. WHO THE HELL ELSE AM I GONNA MARRY? NEXT CHURCH WE COME TO, YOU SUPPLY THE RINGS AND I'LL SORT OUT THE BOOZE.

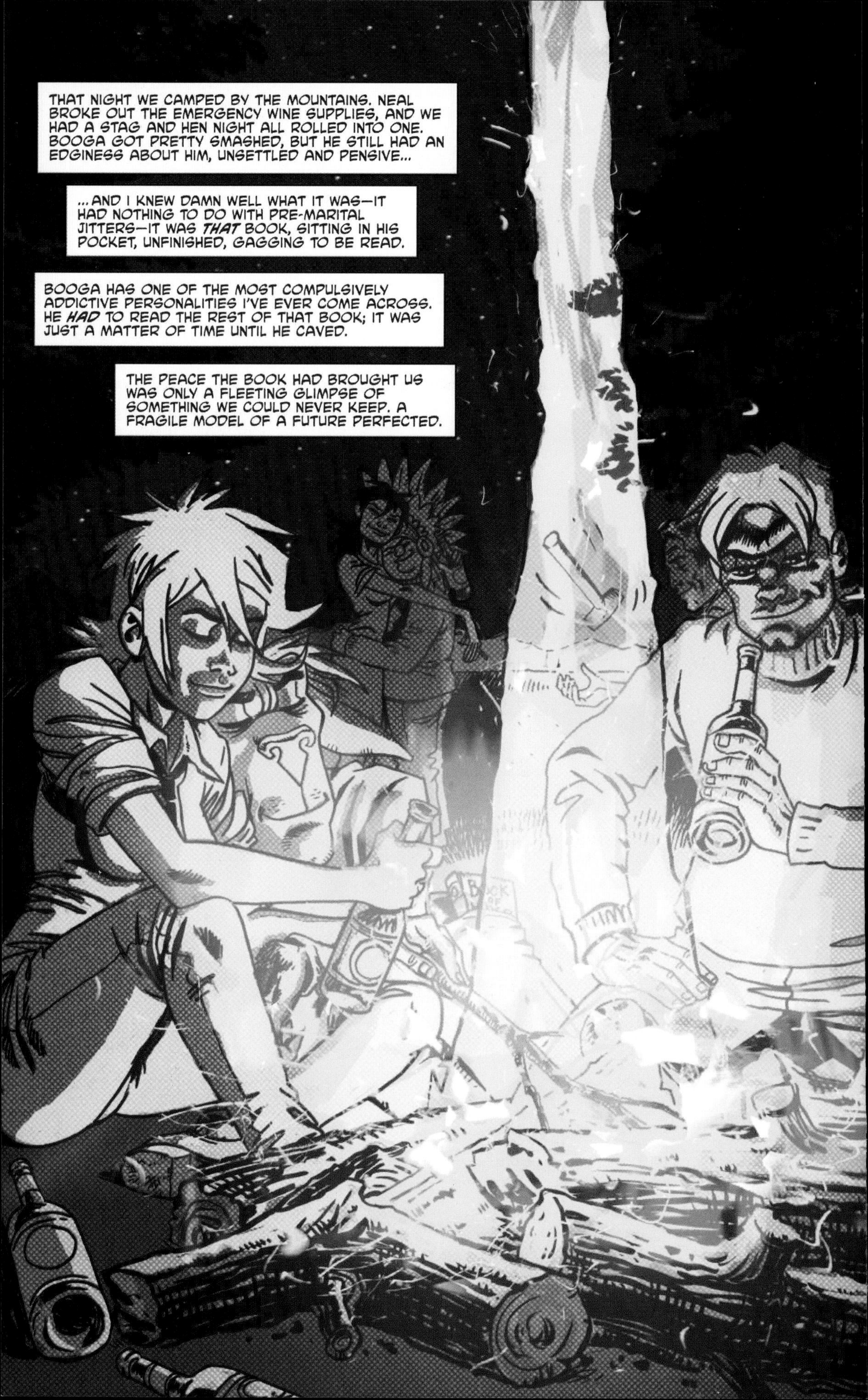
THAT NIGHT WE CAMPED BY THE MOUNTAINS. NEAL BROKE OUT THE EMERGENCY WINE SUPPLIES, AND WE HAD A STAG AND HEN NIGHT ALL ROLLED INTO ONE. BOOGA GOT PRETTY SMASHED, BUT HE STILL HAD AN EDGINESS ABOUT HIM, UNSETTLED AND PENSIVE...
...AND I KNEW DAMN WELL WHAT IT WAS—IT HAD NOTHING TO DO WITH PRE-MARITAL JITTERS—IT WAS *THAT* BOOK, SITTING IN HIS POCKET, UNFINISHED, GAGGING TO BE READ.
BOOGA HAS ONE OF THE MOST COMPULSIVELY ADDICTIVE PERSONALITIES I'VE EVER COME ACROSS. HE *HAD* TO READ THE REST OF THAT BOOK; IT WAS JUST A MATTER OF TIME UNTIL HE CAVED.
THE PEACE THE BOOK HAD BROUGHT US WAS ONLY A FLEETING GLIMPSE OF SOMETHING WE COULD NEVER KEEP. A FRAGILE MODEL OF A FUTURE PERFECTED.

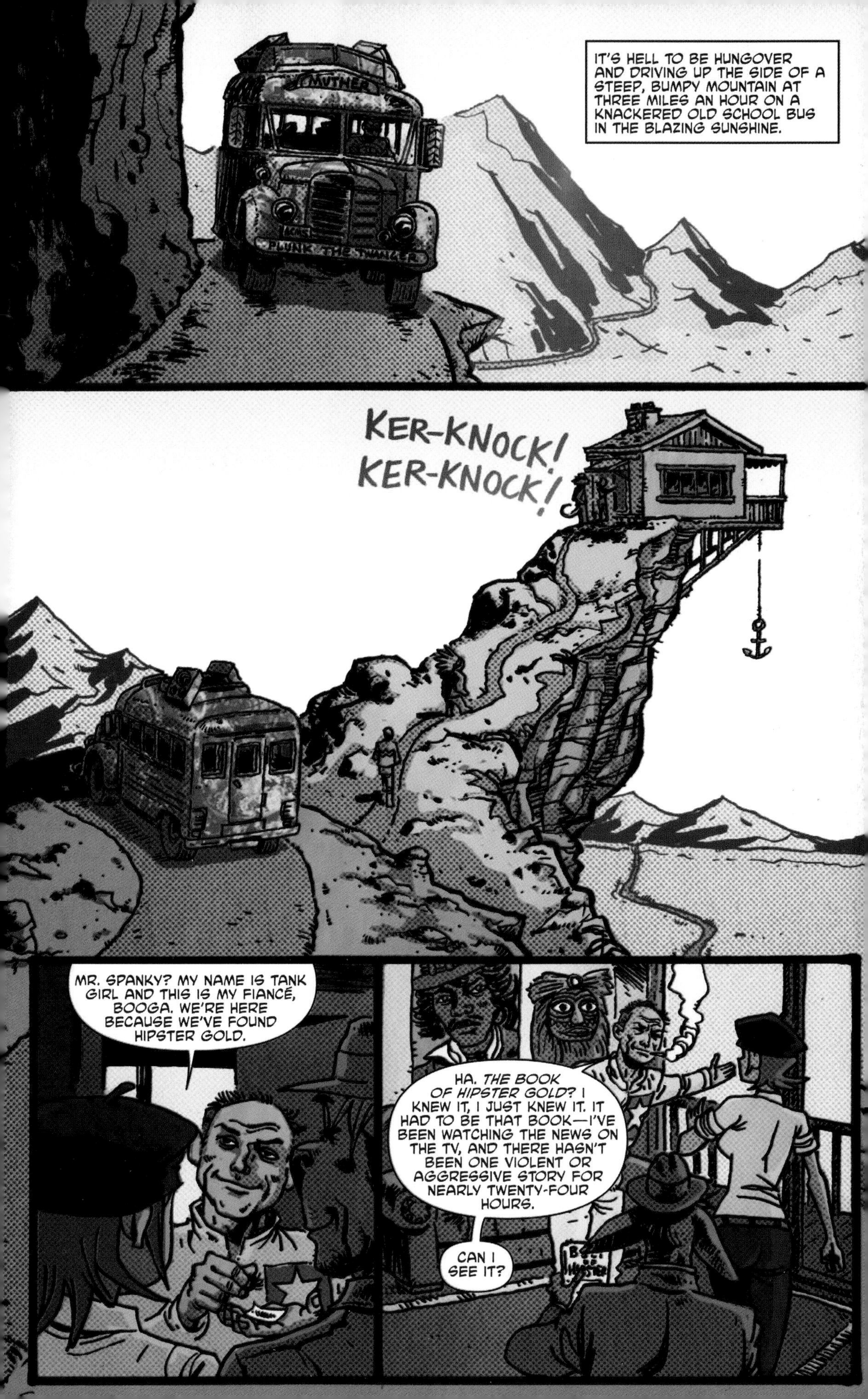
IT'S HELL TO BE HUNGOVER AND DRIVING UP THE SIDE OF A STEEP, BUMPY MOUNTAIN AT THREE MILES AN HOUR ON A KNACKERED OLD SCHOOL BUS IN THE BLAZING SUNSHINE.
KER-KNOCK!
KER-KNOCK!
MR. SPANKY? MY NAME IS TANK GIRL AND THIS IS MY FIANCÉ, BOOGA. WE'RE HERE BECAUSE WE'VE FOUND HIPSTER GOLD.
HA. *THE BOOK OF HIPSTER GOLD?* I KNEW IT, I JUST KNEW IT. IT HAD TO BE THAT BOOK—I'VE BEEN WATCHING THE NEWS ON THE TV, AND THERE HASN'T BEEN ONE VIOLENT OR AGGRESSIVE STORY FOR NEARLY TWENTY-FOUR HOURS.
CAN I SEE IT?

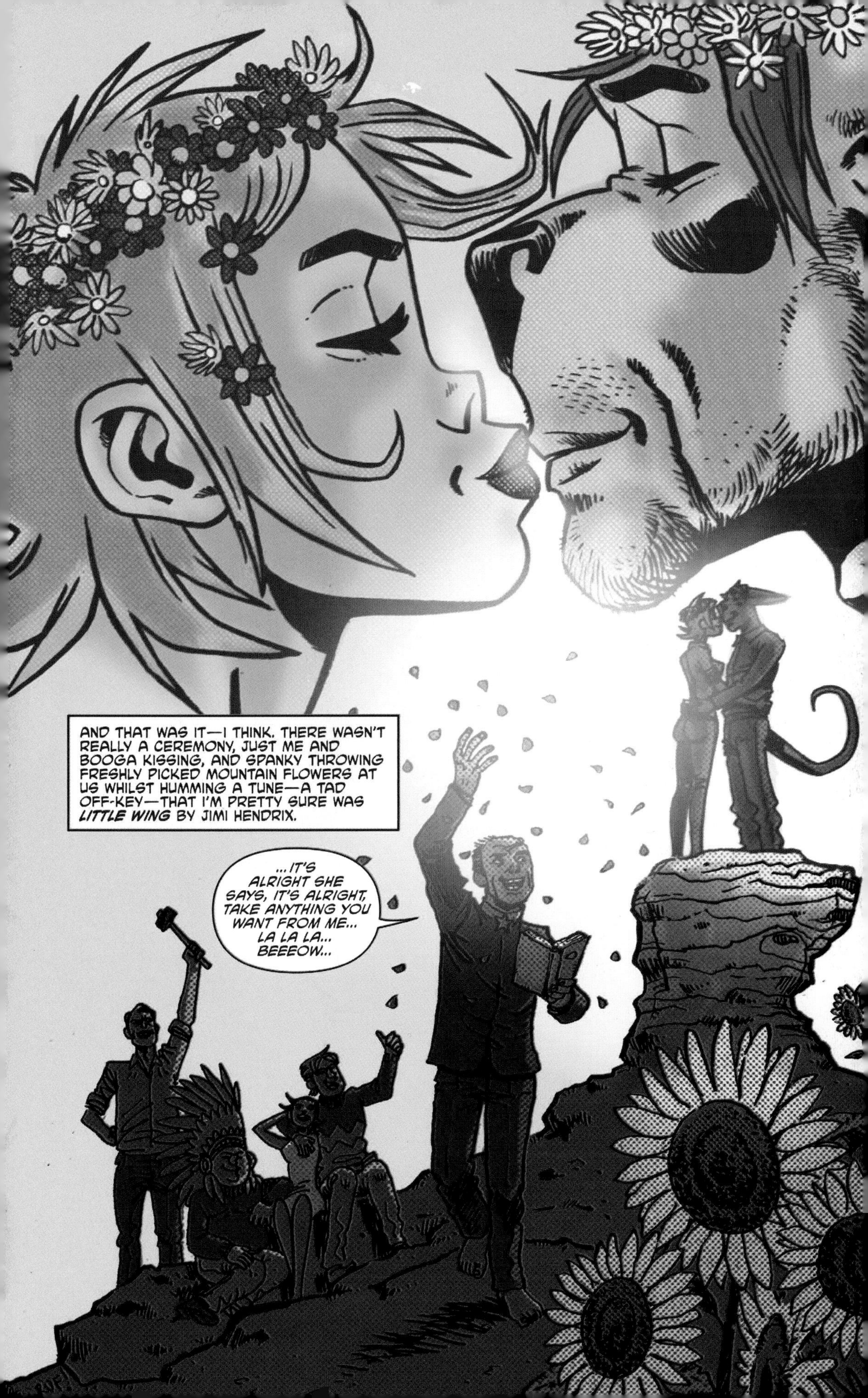
AND THAT WAS IT—I THINK. THERE WASN'T REALLY A CEREMONY, JUST ME AND BOOGA KISSING, AND SPANKY THROWING FRESHLY PICKED MOUNTAIN FLOWERS AT US WHILST HUMMING A TUNE—A TAD OFF-KEY—THAT I'M PRETTY SURE WAS *LITTLE WING* BY JIMI HENDRIX.
...IT'S ALRIGHT SHE SAYS, IT'S ALRIGHT, TAKE ANYTHING YOU WANT FROM ME... LA LA LA... BEEEOW...

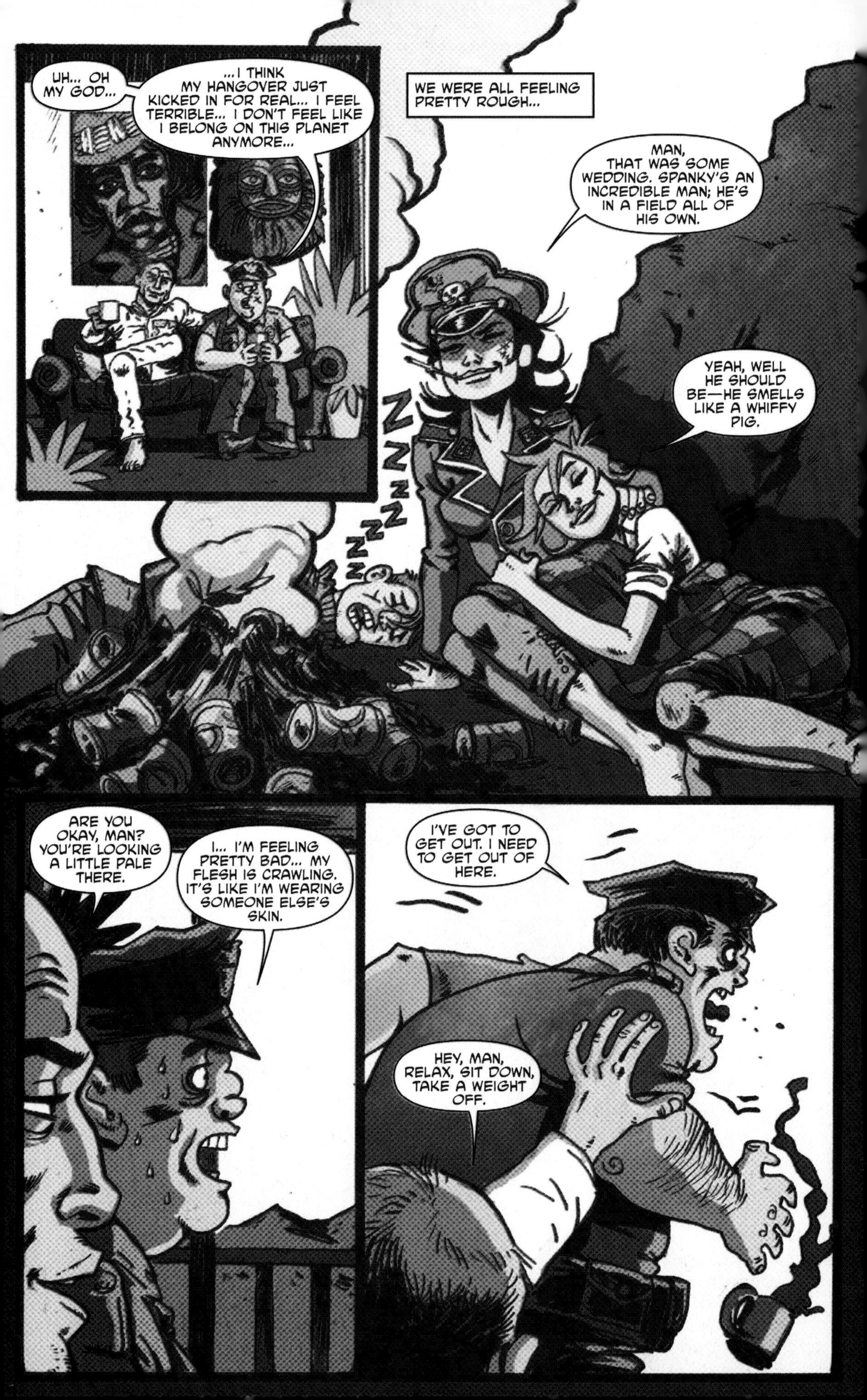
UH... OH MY GOD...
...I THINK MY HANGOVER JUST KICKED IN FOR REAL... I FEEL TERRIBLE... I DON'T FEEL LIKE I BELONG ON THIS PLANET ANYMORE...
WE WERE ALL FEELING PRETTY ROUGH...
MAN, THAT WAS SOME WEDDING. SPANKY'S AN INCREDIBLE MAN; HE'S IN A FIELD ALL OF HIS OWN.
YEAH, WELL HE SHOULD BE—HE SMELLS LIKE A WHIFFY PIG.
ZZZZZ
ARE YOU OKAY, MAN? YOU'RE LOOKING A LITTLE PALE THERE.
I... I'M FEELING PRETTY BAD... MY FLESH IS CRAWLING. IT'S LIKE I'M WEARING SOMEONE ELSE'S SKIN.
I'VE GOT TO GET OUT. I NEED TO GET OUT OF HERE.
HEY, MAN, RELAX, SIT DOWN, TAKE A WEIGHT OFF.

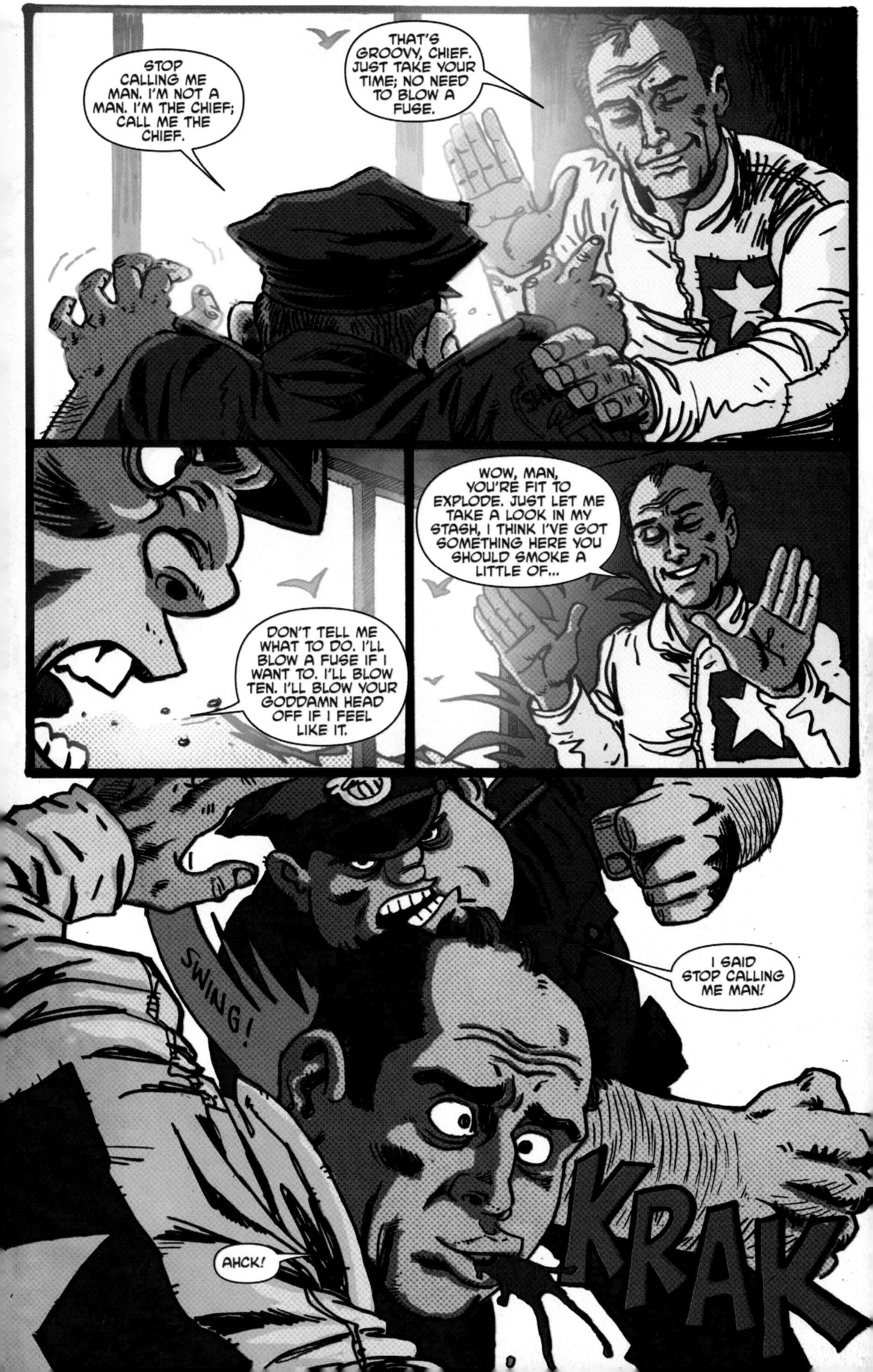
STOP CALLING ME MAN. I'M NOT A MAN. I'M THE CHIEF; CALL ME THE CHIEF.
THAT'S GROOVY, CHIEF. JUST TAKE YOUR TIME; NO NEED TO BLOW A FUSE.
DON'T TELL ME WHAT TO DO. I'LL BLOW A FUSE IF I WANT TO. I'LL BLOW TEN. I'LL BLOW YOUR GODDAMN HEAD OFF IF I FEEL LIKE IT.
WOW, MAN, YOU'RE FIT TO EXPLODE. JUST LET ME TAKE A LOOK IN MY STASH, I THINK I'VE GOT SOMETHING HERE YOU SHOULD SMOKE A LITTLE OF...
SWING!
I SAID STOP CALLING ME MAN!
AHCK!
KRAK

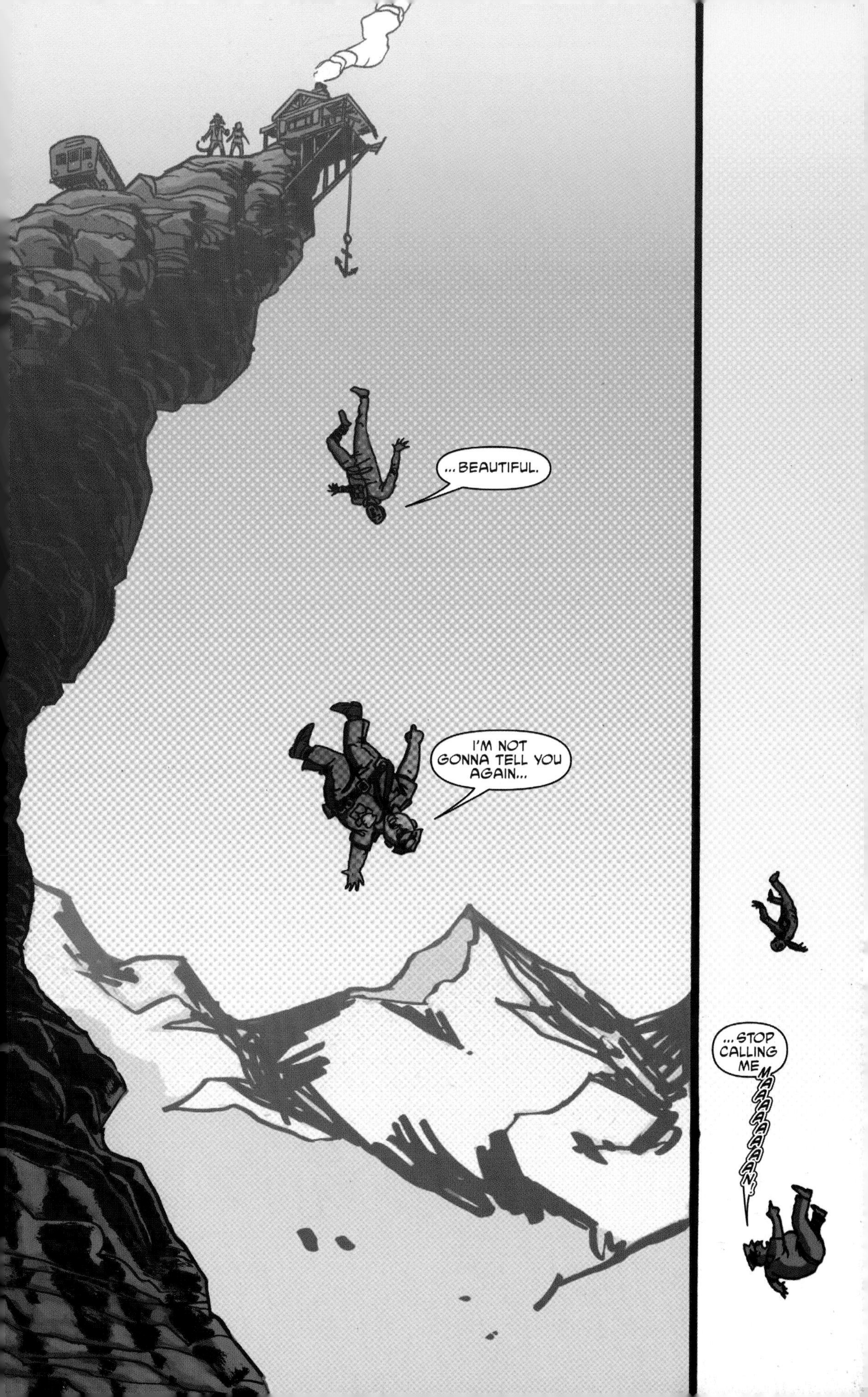
...BEAUTIFUL.
I'M NOT GONNA TELL YOU AGAIN...
...STOP CALLING ME MAAAAAAAAAN!

SUNNY BAY—A HAVEN, AN ESCAPE, A PARADISE.
IF YOU DRIVE ACROSS THE COUNTRY TO THE WEST
COAST, THIS IS WHERE YOU'LL END UP. YOU CAN
GO NO FARTHER, AND WHY THE HELL WOULD YOU
WANT TO? PEOPLE COME TO HOLIDAY, GAMBLE,
RETIRE, PARTY, RACE YACHTS, AND DRINK FANCY
COCKTAILS THROUGH NOVELTY STRAWS.

OUR NEW FRIEND NEAL HAD DRIVEN US FOR
SIX DAYS STRAIGHT, STOPPING ONLY FOR
BURGERS, GAS, AND POO-CALLS. WE HAD
KILLED A MAFIA BOSS AND A POLICE
CHIEF—WHO JUST SO HAPPENED TO BE
BROTHERS. A THIRD BROTHER WAS HOT ON
OUR HEELS WITH A RABID THIRST FOR
REVENGE AND AN ARMY OF GORE-HUNGRY
HENCHMEN IN TOW.

TANK GIRL
VISIONS OF BOOGA
PART 4
WHICH CUTS THE FINEST THE SABRE, OR THE BLADE OF GRASS?
BY ALAN AND RUFUS

SPLISH SPLOSH!

BOOGA HAD DISCOVERED THAT HE
HAD A LONG-LOST SIBLING IN SUNNY
BAY, AND WE'D COME LOOKING FOR
HIM, THINKING THAT HE COULD
SUPPLY US WITH A LUXURY HIDEOUT.

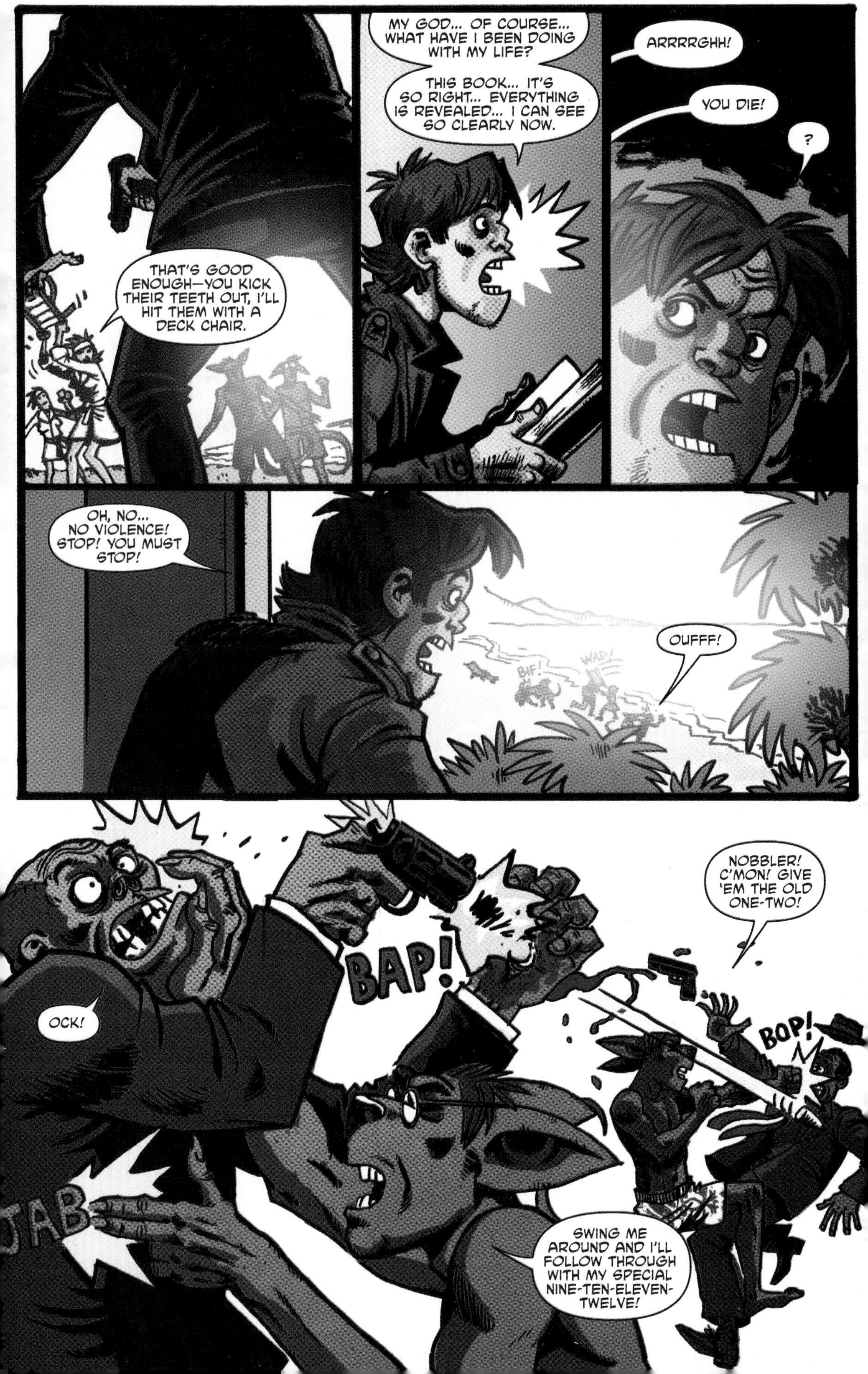
THAT'S GOOD ENOUGH—YOU KICK THEIR TEETH OUT, I'LL HIT THEM WITH A DECK CHAIR.
MY GOD... OF COURSE... WHAT HAVE I BEEN DOING WITH MY LIFE?
THIS BOOK... IT'S SO RIGHT... EVERYTHING IS REVEALED... I CAN SEE SO CLEARLY NOW.
ARRRRGHH!
YOU DIE!
?
OH, NO... NO VIOLENCE! STOP! YOU MUST STOP!
BIF!
WAP!
OUFFF!
BAP!
OCK!
NOBBLER! C'MON! GIVE 'EM THE OLD ONE-TWO!
BOP!
JAB
SWING ME AROUND AND I'LL FOLLOW THROUGH WITH MY SPECIAL NINE-TEN-ELEVEN-TWELVE!

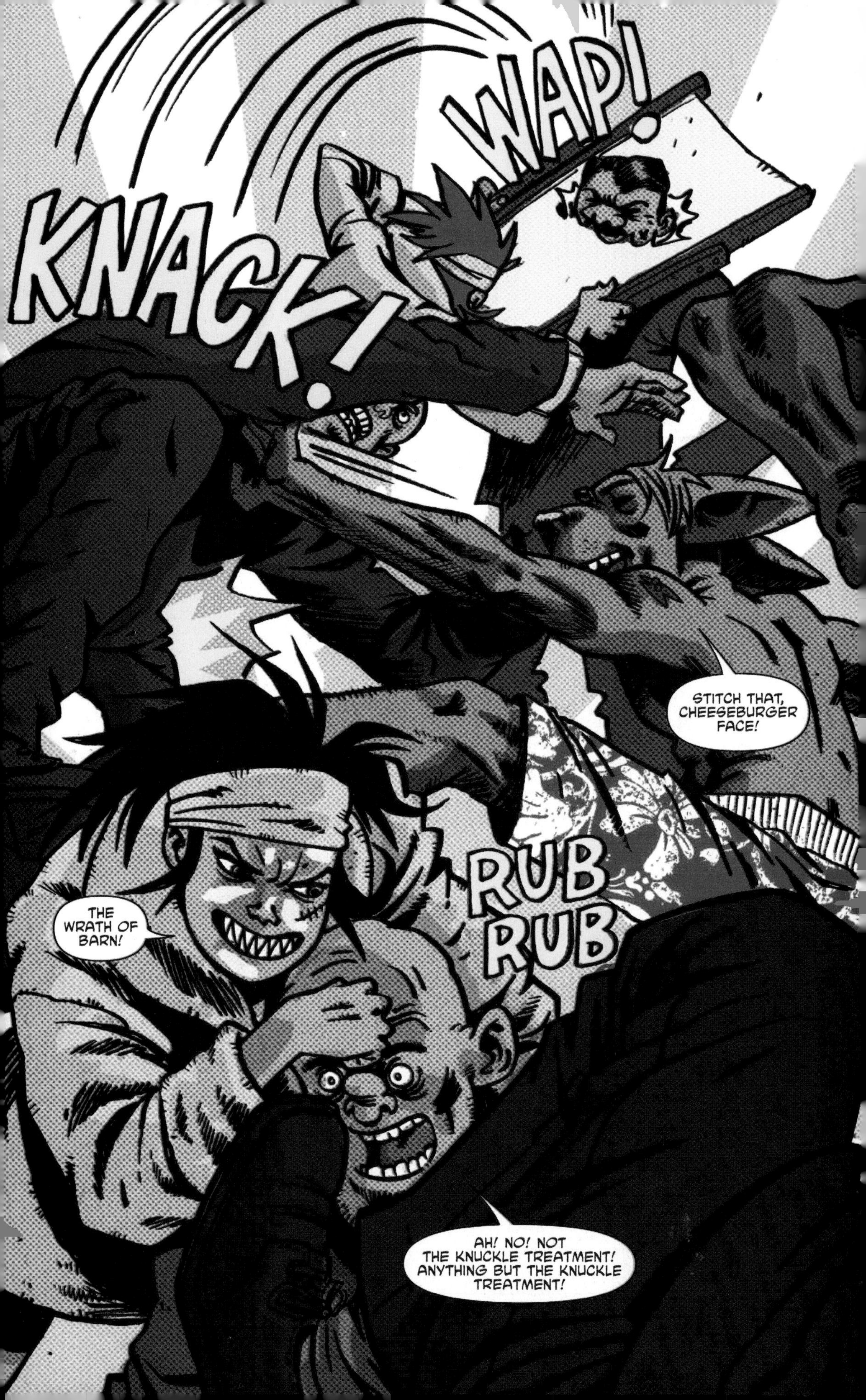
WAP!
KNACK!
STITCH THAT, CHEESEBURGER FACE!
RUB RUB
THE WRATH OF BARN!
AH! NO! NOT THE KNUCKLE TREATMENT! ANYTHING BUT THE KNUCKLE TREATMENT!

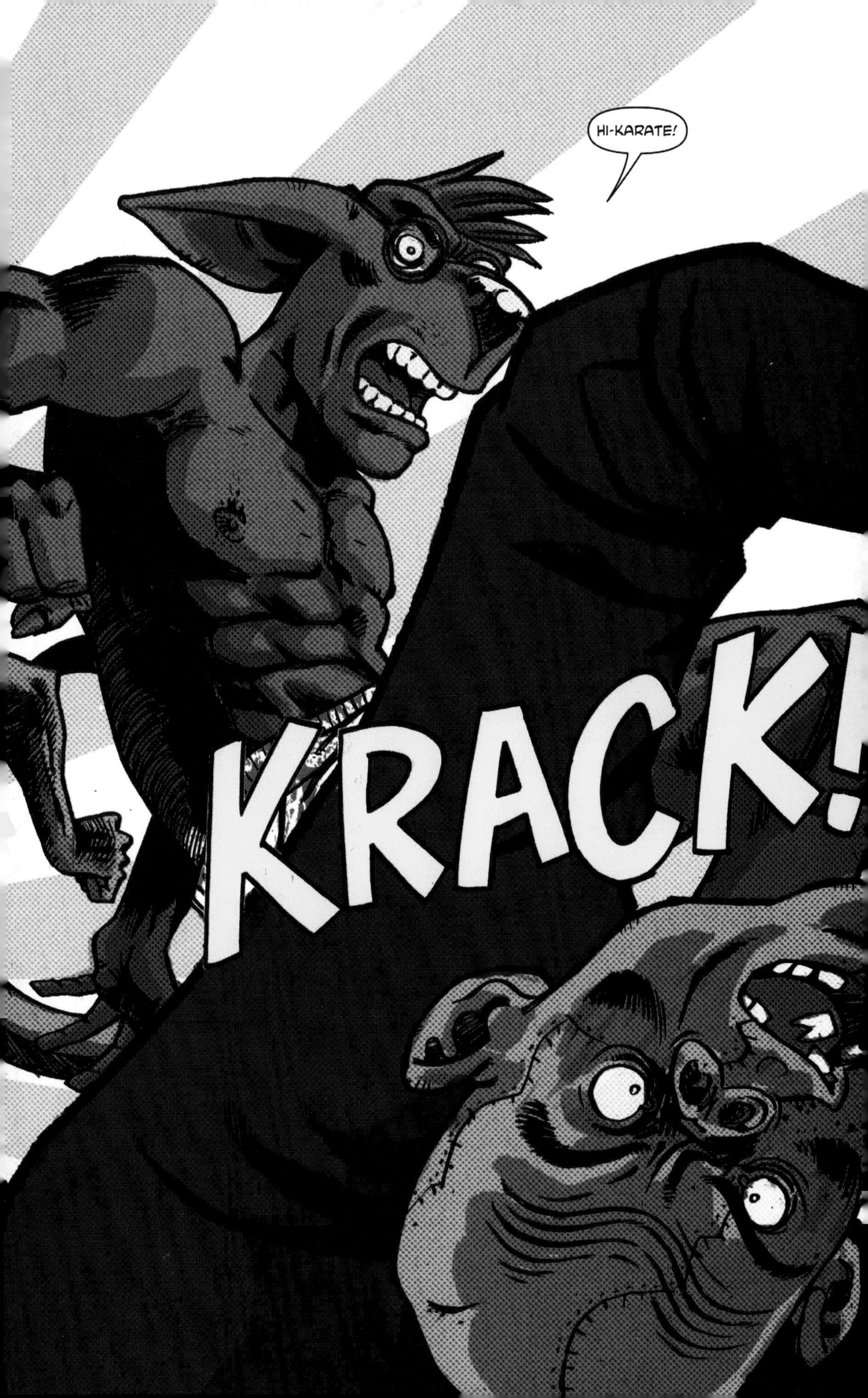
HI-KARATE!
KRACK!

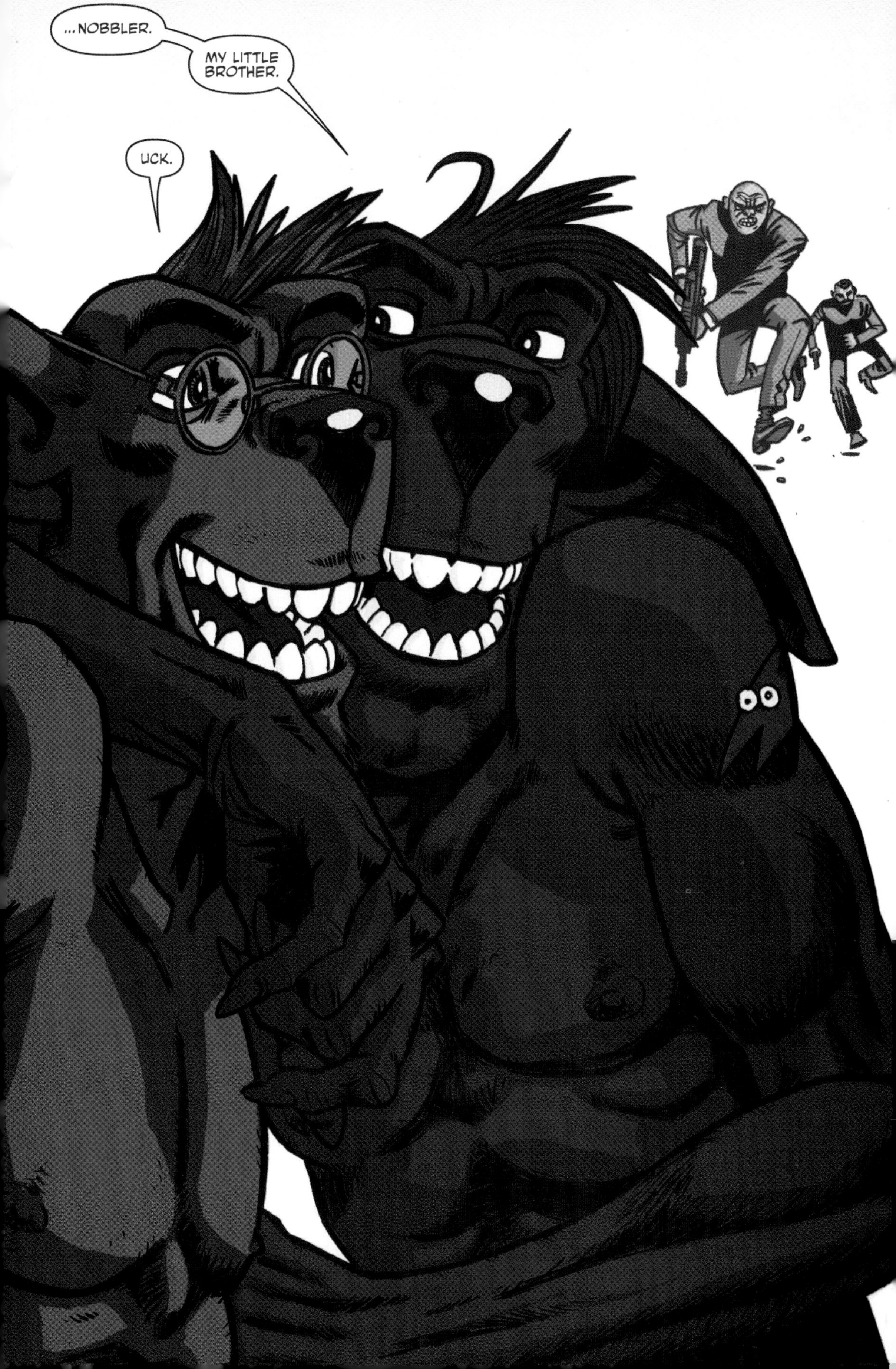
...NOBBLER.
MY LITTLE BROTHER.
UCK.

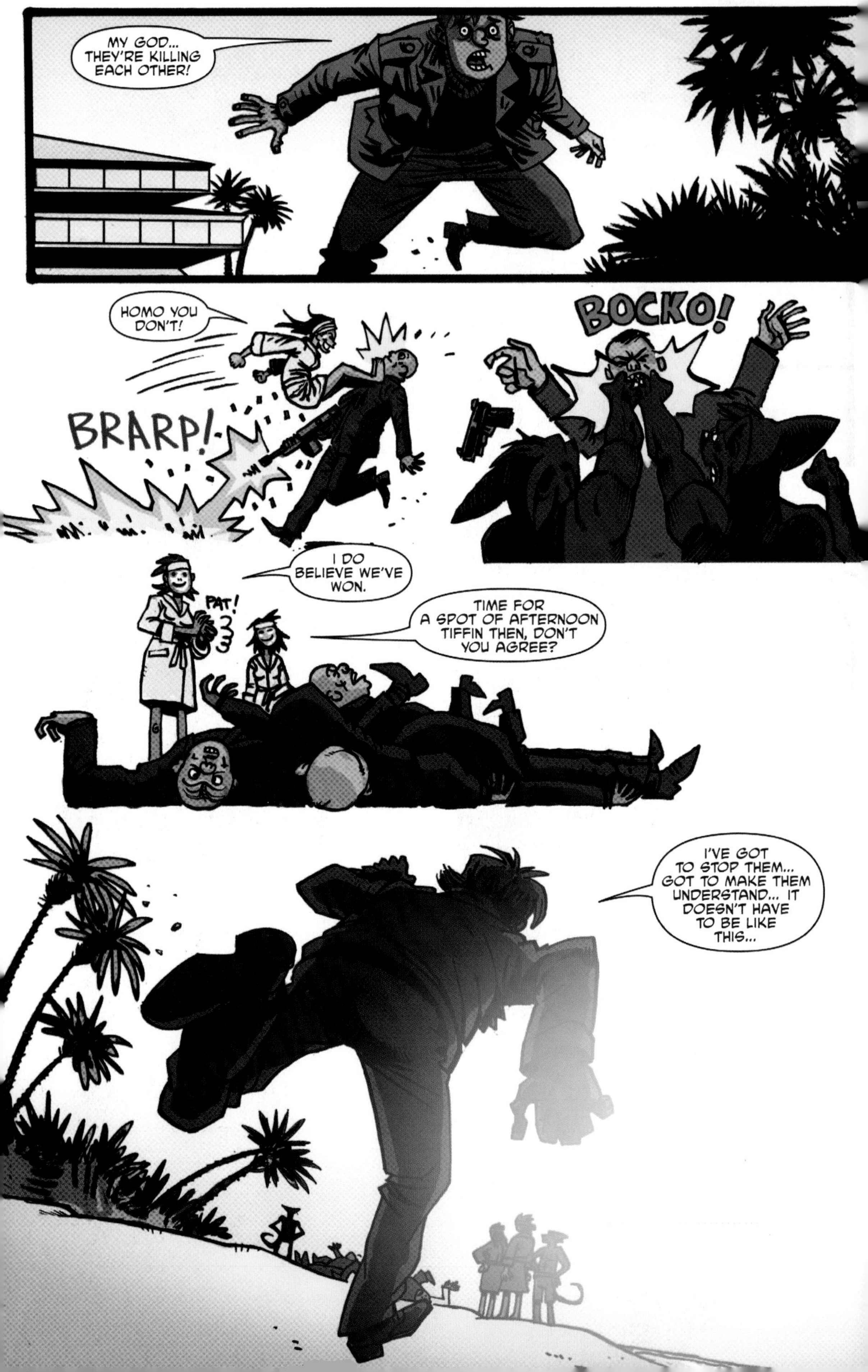
MY GOD... THEY'RE KILLING EACH OTHER!
HOMO YOU DON'T!
BRARP!
BOCKO!
I DO BELIEVE WE'VE WON.
PAT!
TIME FOR A SPOT OF AFTERNOON TIFFIN THEN, DON'T YOU AGREE?
I'VE GOT TO STOP THEM... GOT TO MAKE THEM UNDERSTAND... IT DOESN'T HAVE TO BE LIKE THIS...

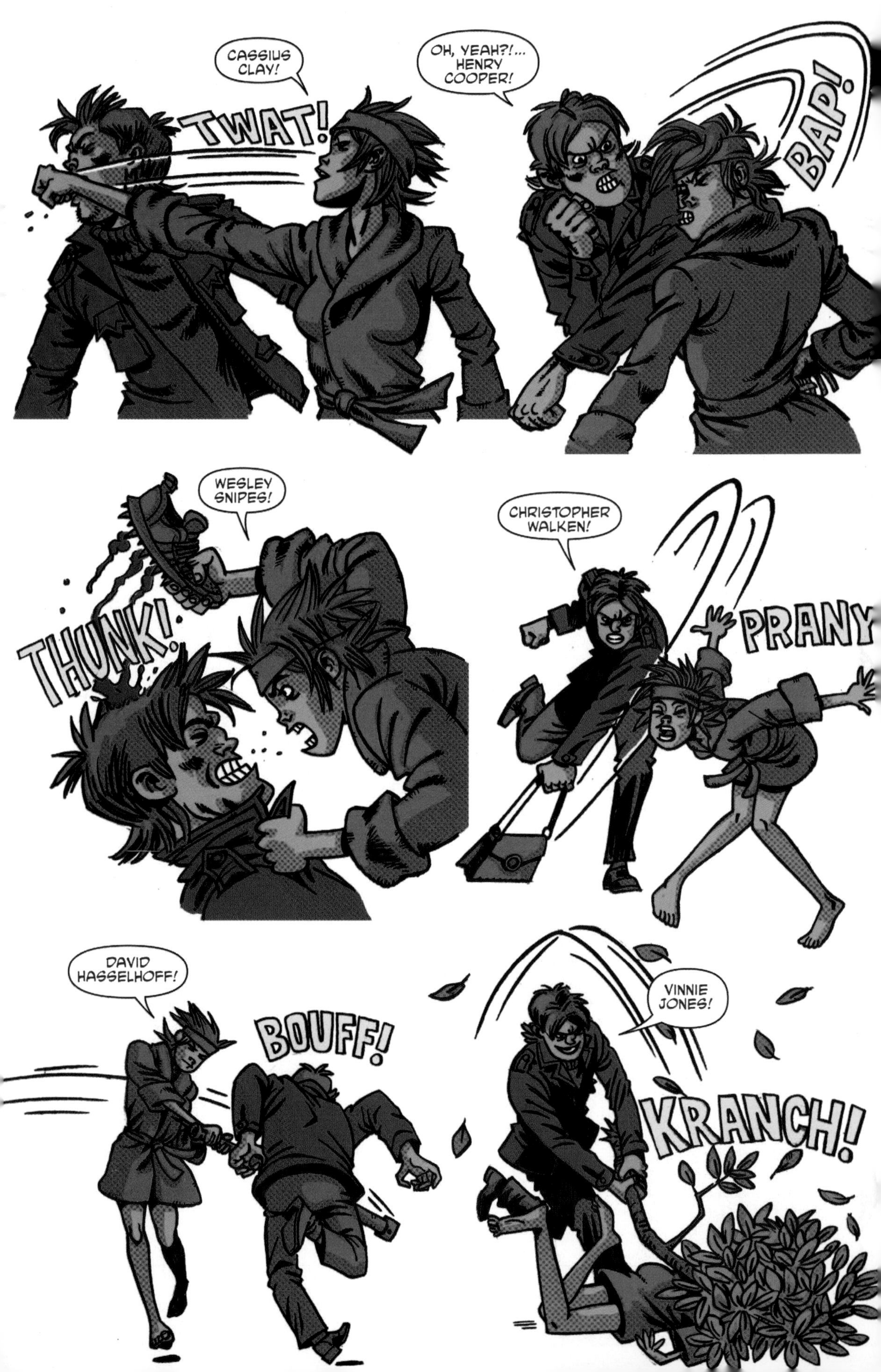
CASSIUS CLAY!
TWAT!
OH, YEAH?!... HENRY COOPER!
BAP!
WESLEY SNIPES!
THUNK!
CHRISTOPHER WALKEN!
PRANY
DAVID HASSELHOFF!
BOUFF!
VINNIE JONES!
KRANCH!

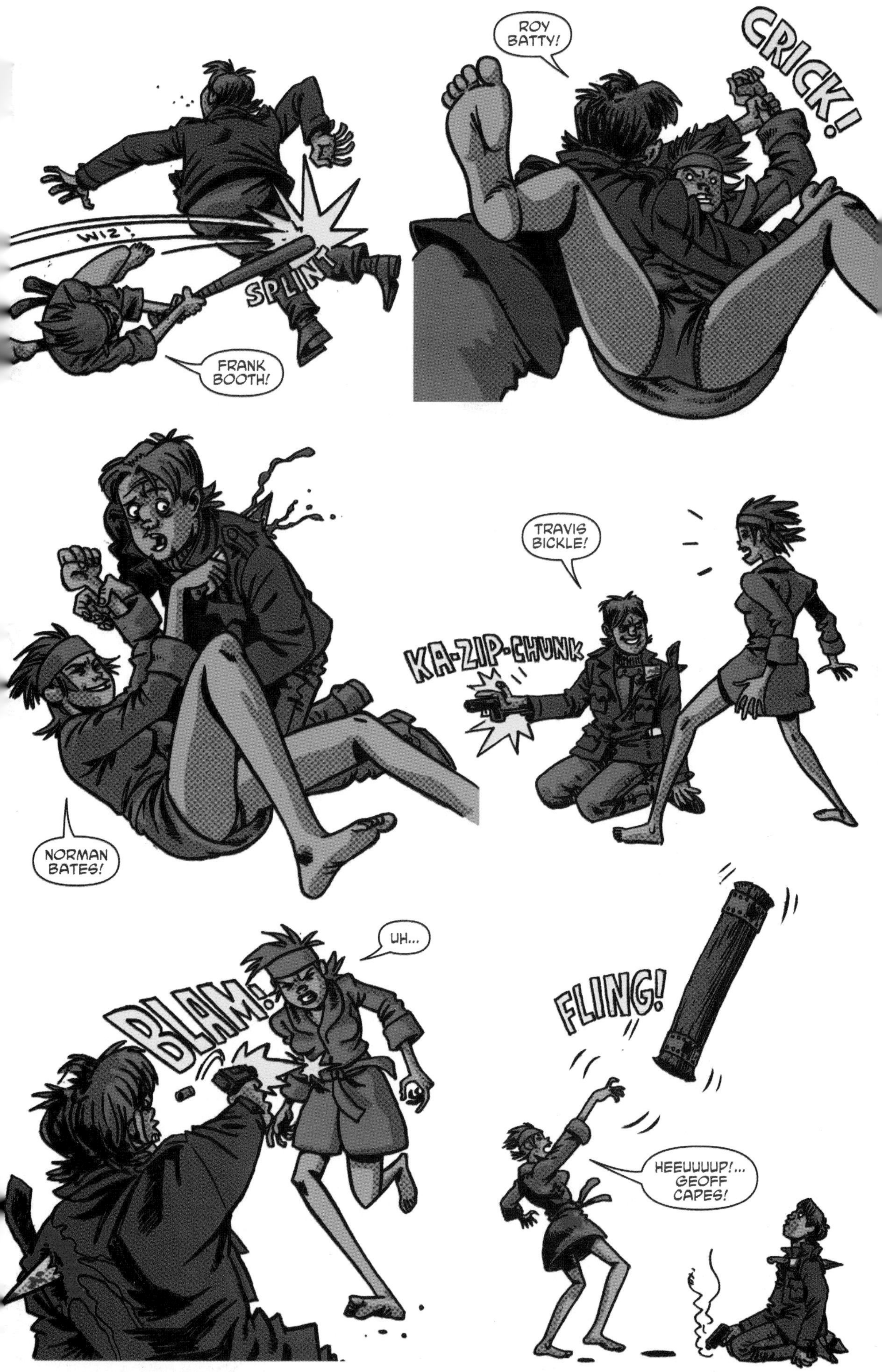
WIZ!
SPLINT
FRANK BOOTH!
ROY BATTY!
CRICK!
NORMAN BATES!
TRAVIS BICKLE!
KA-ZIP-CHUNK
UH...
BLAM!
FLING!
HEEUUUUP!... GEOFF CAPES!

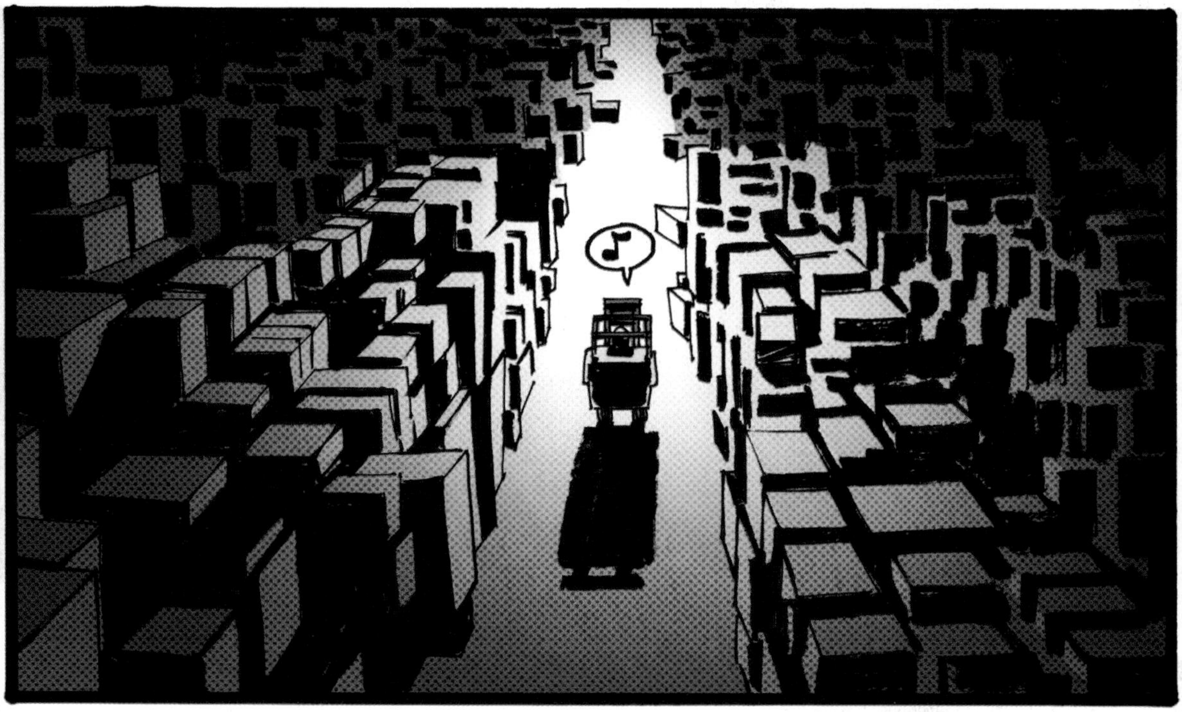

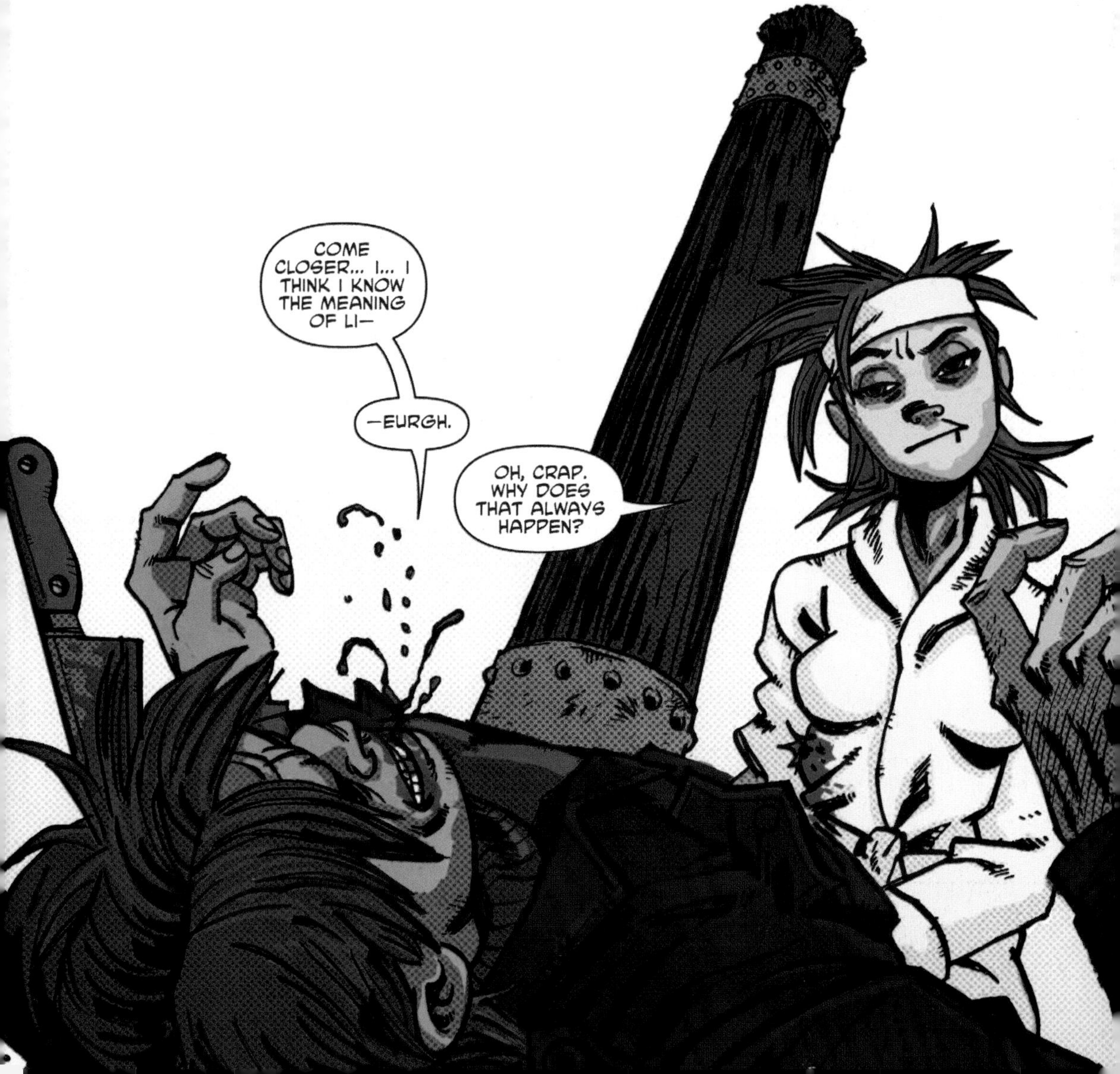
COME CLOSER... I... I THINK I KNOW THE MEANING OF LI—
—EURGH.
OH, CRAP. WHY DOES THAT ALWAYS HAPPEN?

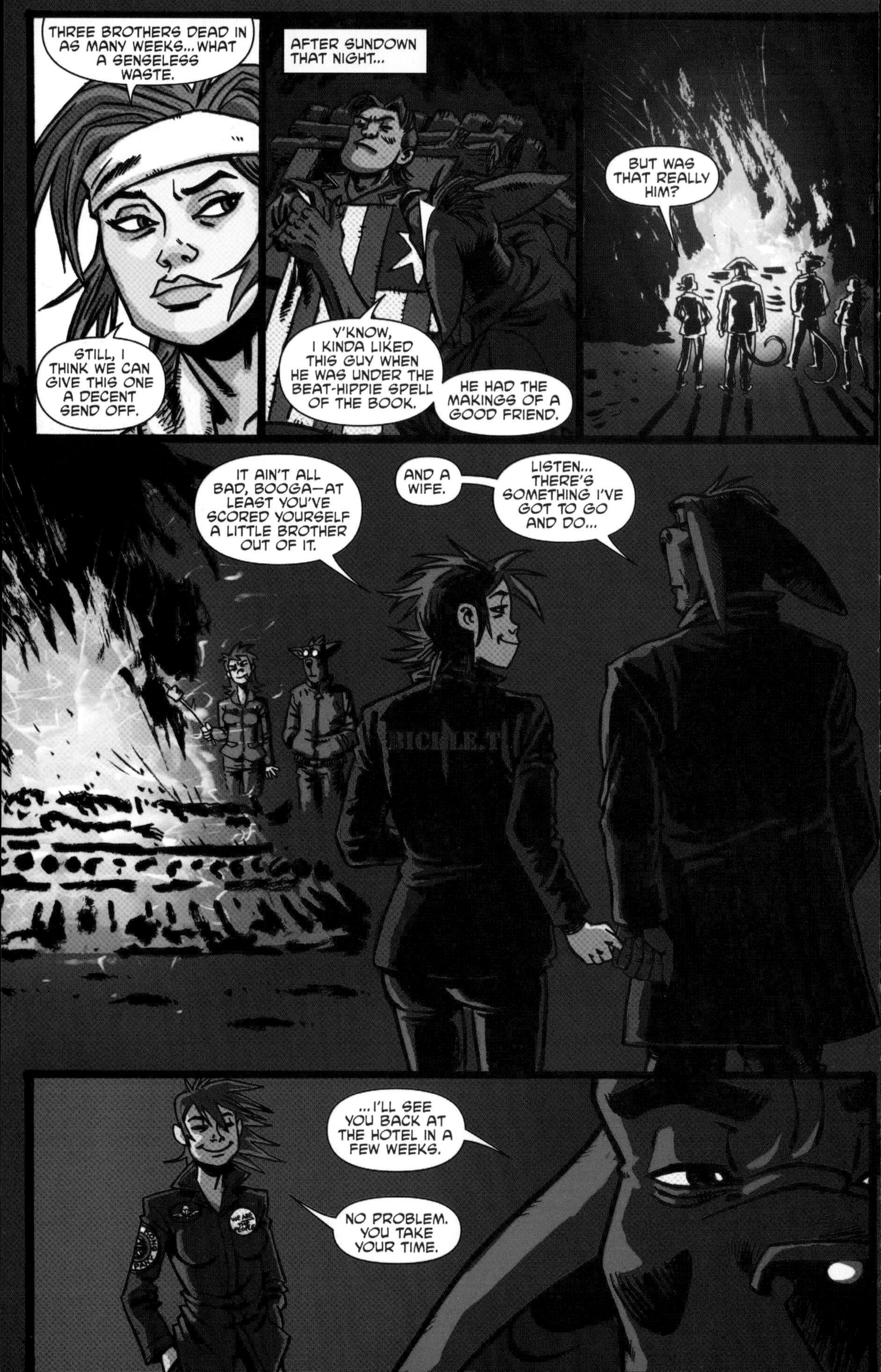
THREE BROTHERS DEAD IN AS MANY WEEKS... WHAT A SENSELESS WASTE.
STILL, I THINK WE CAN GIVE THIS ONE A DECENT SEND OFF.
AFTER SUNDOWN THAT NIGHT...
Y'KNOW, I KINDA LIKED THIS GUY WHEN HE WAS UNDER THE BEAT-HIPPIE SPELL OF THE BOOK.
HE HAD THE MAKINGS OF A GOOD FRIEND.
BUT WAS THAT REALLY HIM?
IT AIN'T ALL BAD, BOOGA—AT LEAST YOU'VE SCORED YOURSELF A LITTLE BROTHER OUT OF IT.
AND A WIFE.
LISTEN... THERE'S SOMETHING I'VE GOT TO GO AND DO...
...I'LL SEE YOU BACK AT THE HOTEL IN A FEW WEEKS.
NO PROBLEM. YOU TAKE YOUR TIME.

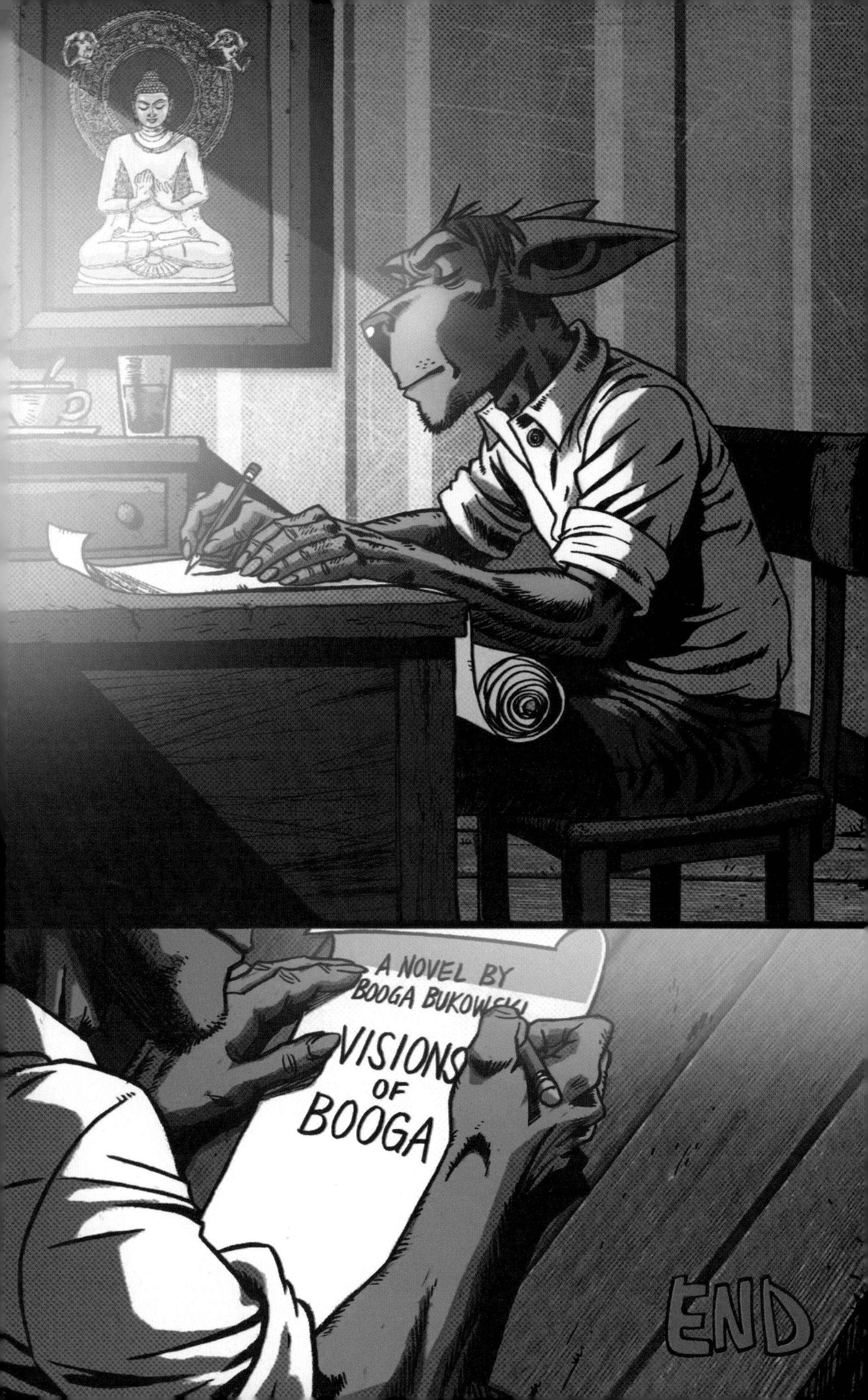
A NOVEL BY
BOOGA BUKOWSKI
VISIONS
OF
BOOGA
END

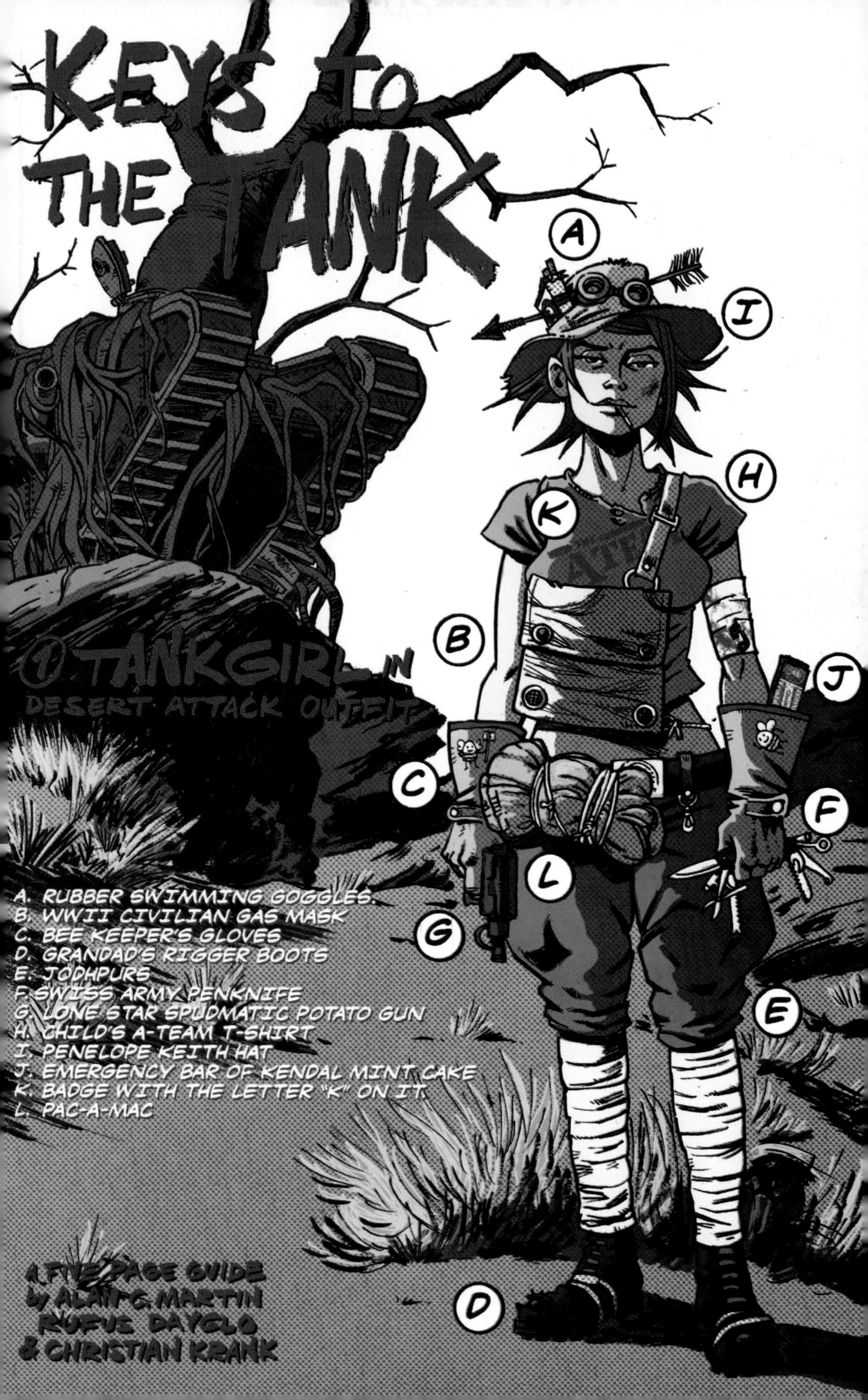
KEYS TO THE TANK
A
I
H
K
B
1 TANKGIRL IN
DESERT ATTACK OUTFIT
J
C
F
L
G
E
D
A. RUBBER SWIMMING GOGGLES.
B. WWII CIVILIAN GAS MASK
C. BEE KEEPER'S GLOVES
D. GRANDAD'S RIGGER BOOTS
E. JODHPURS
F. SWISS ARMY PENKNIFE
G. LONE STAR SPUDMATIC POTATO GUN
H. CHILD'S A-TEAM T-SHIRT
I. PENELOPE KEITH HAT
J. EMERGENCY BAR OF KENDAL MINT CAKE
K. BADGE WITH THE LETTER "K" ON IT.
L. PAC-A-MAC
A FIVE PAGE GUIDE
by ALAN C. MARTIN
RUFUS DAYGLO
& CHRISTIAN KRANK

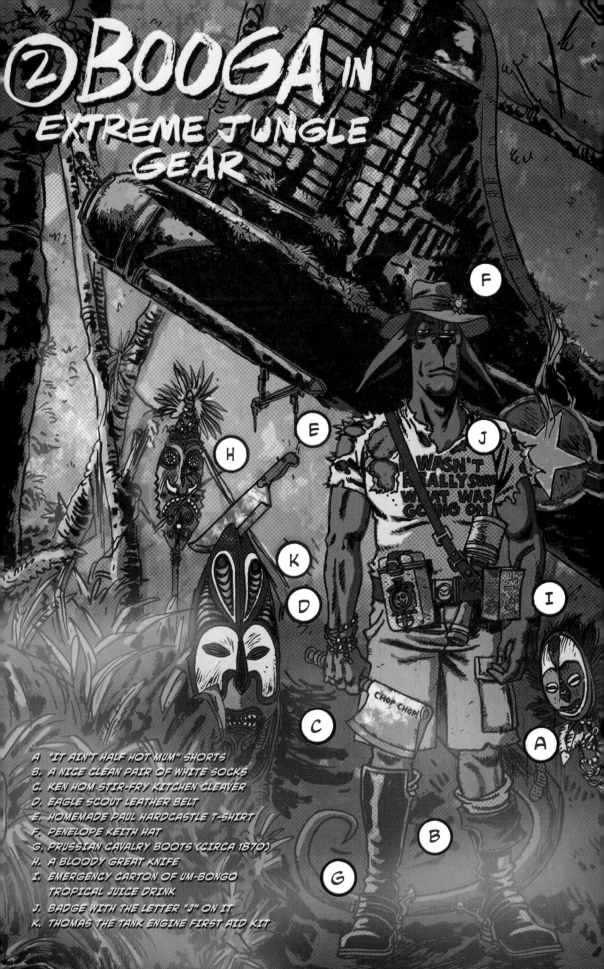

② BOOGA IN EXTREME JUNGLE GEAR

A. "IT AIN'T HALF HOT MUM" SHORTS
B. A NICE CLEAN PAIR OF WHITE SOCKS
C. KEN HOM STIR-FRY KITCHEN CLEAVER
D. EAGLE SCOUT LEATHER BELT
E. HOMEMADE PAUL HARDCASTLE T-SHIRT
F. PENELOPE KEITH HAT
G. PRUSSIAN CAVALRY BOOTS (CIRCA 1870)
H. A BLOODY GREAT KNIFE
I. EMERGENCY CARTON OF UM-BONGO TROPICAL JUICE DRINK
J. BADGE WITH THE LETTER "J" ON IT
K. THOMAS THE TANK ENGINE FIRST AID KIT

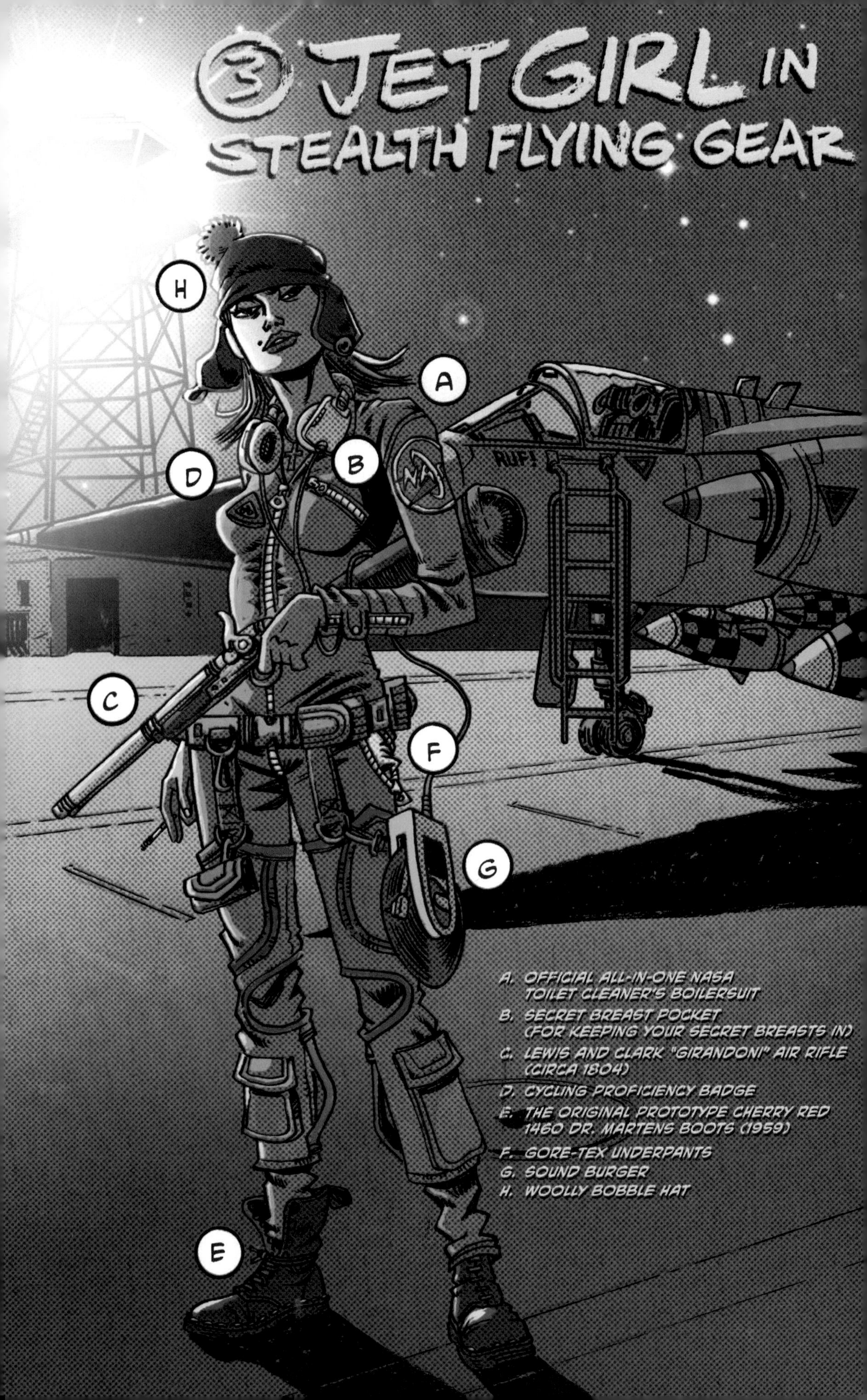

3 JET GIRL IN
STEALTH FLYING GEAR
H
A
D
B
RUF!
C
F
G
E
A. OFFICIAL ALL-IN-ONE NASA TOILET CLEANER'S BOILERSUIT
B. SECRET BREAST POCKET (FOR KEEPING YOUR SECRET BREASTS IN)
C. LEWIS AND CLARK "GIRANDONI" AIR RIFLE (CIRCA 1804)
D. CYCLING PROFICIENCY BADGE
E. THE ORIGINAL PROTOTYPE CHERRY RED 1460 DR. MARTENS BOOTS (1959)
F. GORE-TEX UNDERPANTS
G. SOUND BURGER
H. WOOLLY BOBBLE HAT

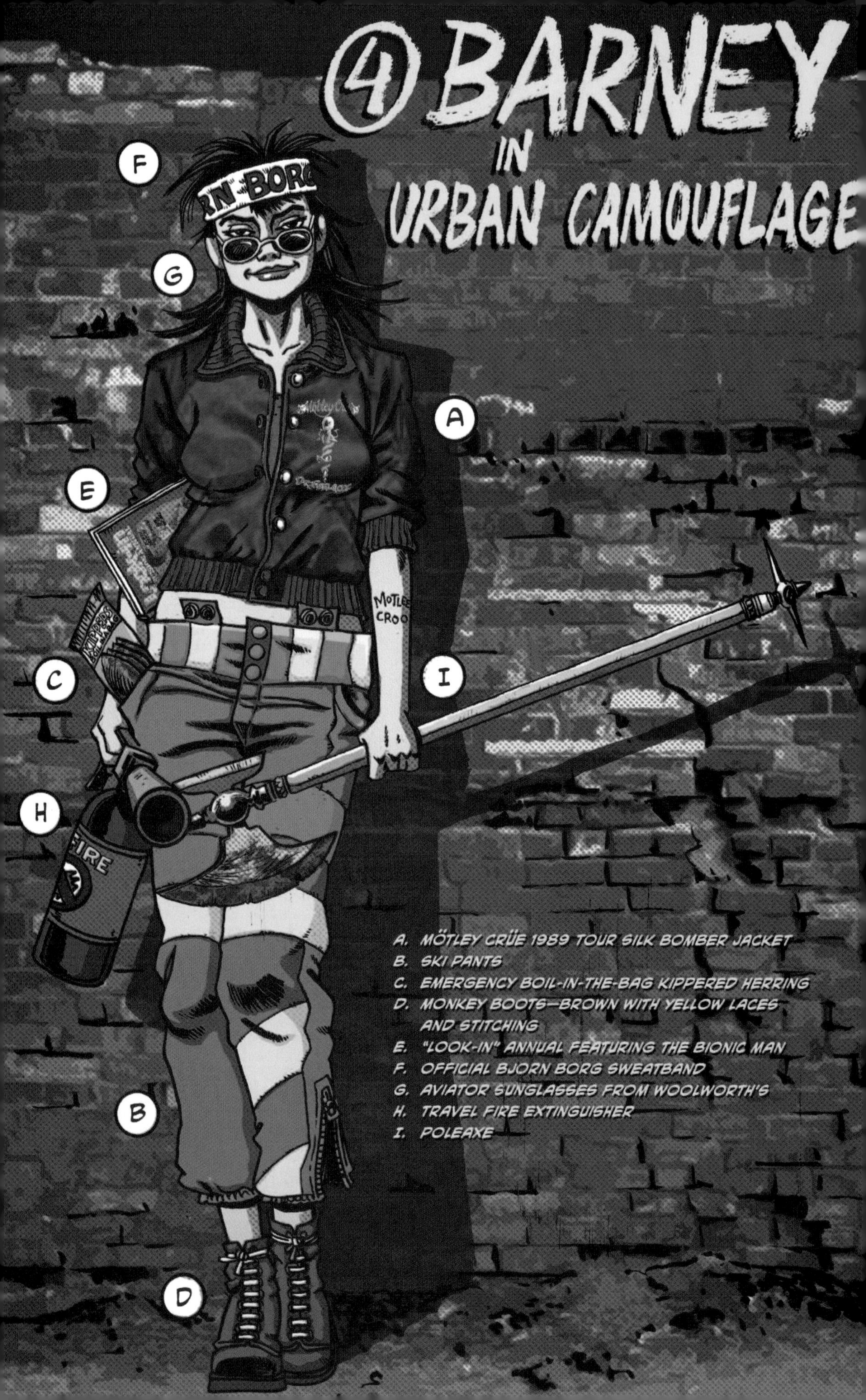
④ BARNEY
IN
URBAN CAMOUFLAGE
F
G
A
E
C
I
H
B
D
MOTLEE CROO
FIRE
A. MÖTLEY CRÜE 1989 TOUR SILK BOMBER JACKET
B. SKI PANTS
C. EMERGENCY BOIL-IN-THE-BAG KIPPERED HERRING
D. MONKEY BOOTS—BROWN WITH YELLOW LACES AND STITCHING
E. "LOOK-IN" ANNUAL FEATURING THE BIONIC MAN
F. OFFICIAL BJORN BORG SWEATBAND
G. AVIATOR SUNGLASSES FROM WOOLWORTH'S
H. TRAVEL FIRE EXTINGUISHER
I. POLEAXE

⑤ CRUISER TANK IN FULL RACING LIVERY

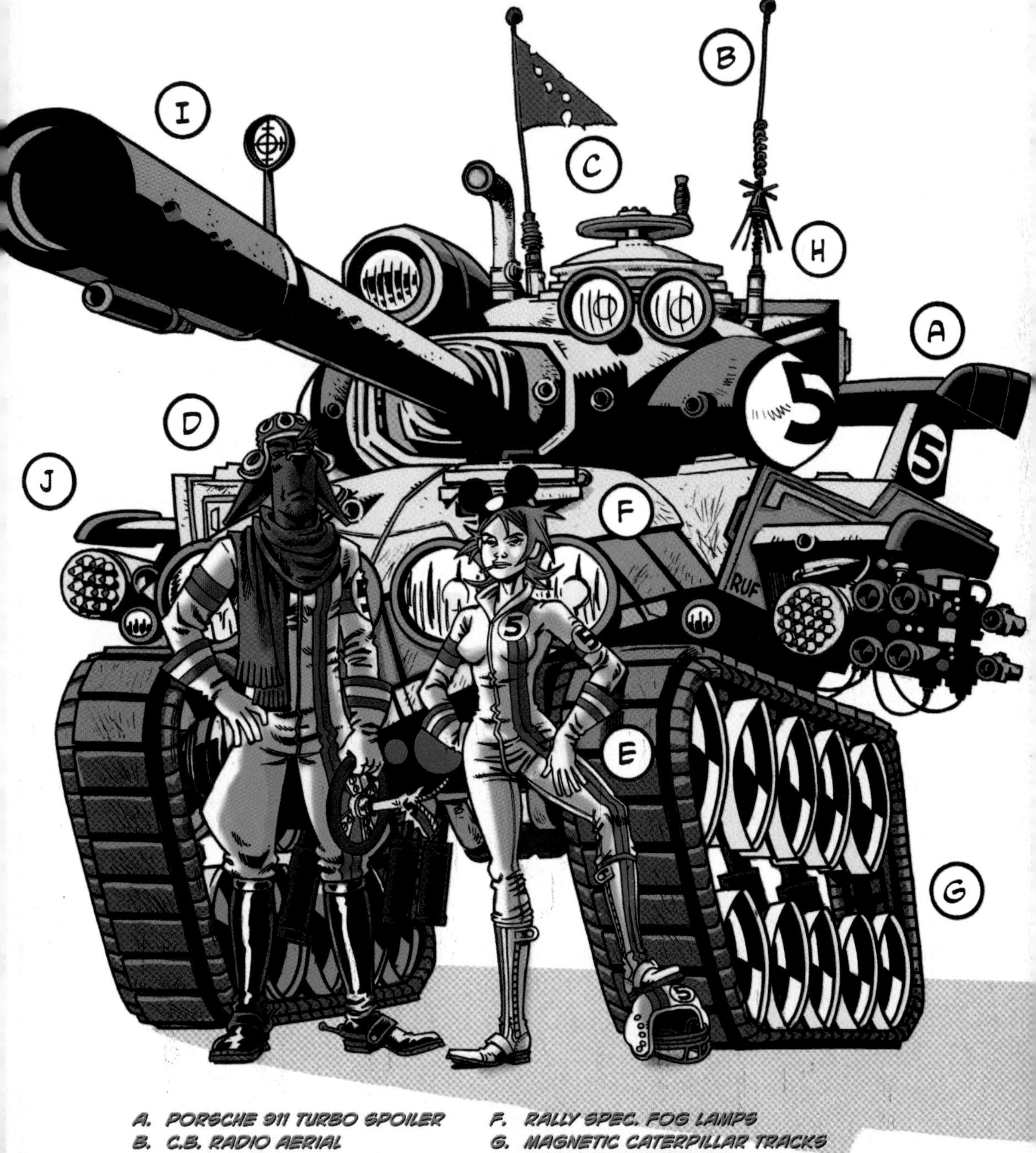

B
I
C
H
A
D
J
F
E
G

A. PORSCHE 911 TURBO SPOILER
B. C.B. RADIO AERIAL
C. THE WAY IN
D. TANK DRIVER
E. NAVIGATOR/MECHANIC
F. RALLY SPEC. FOG LAMPS
G. MAGNETIC CATERPILLAR TRACKS
H. LUNCH COMPARTMENT
I. RE-MODELED 8.8 CM KAMPFWAGENKANONE 36 L/56 CANNON FROM A TIGER1 TANK
J. FIZZBOMBS

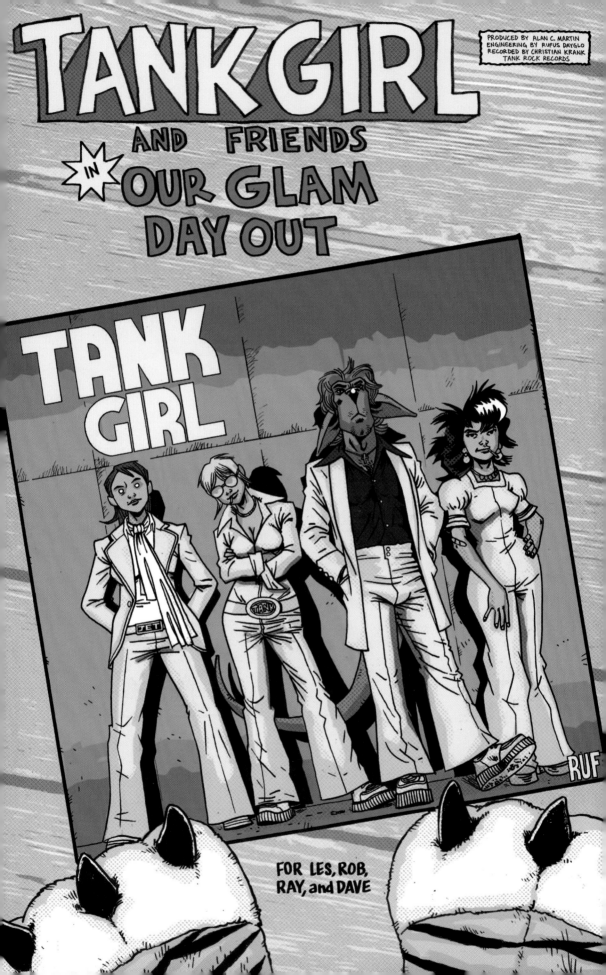

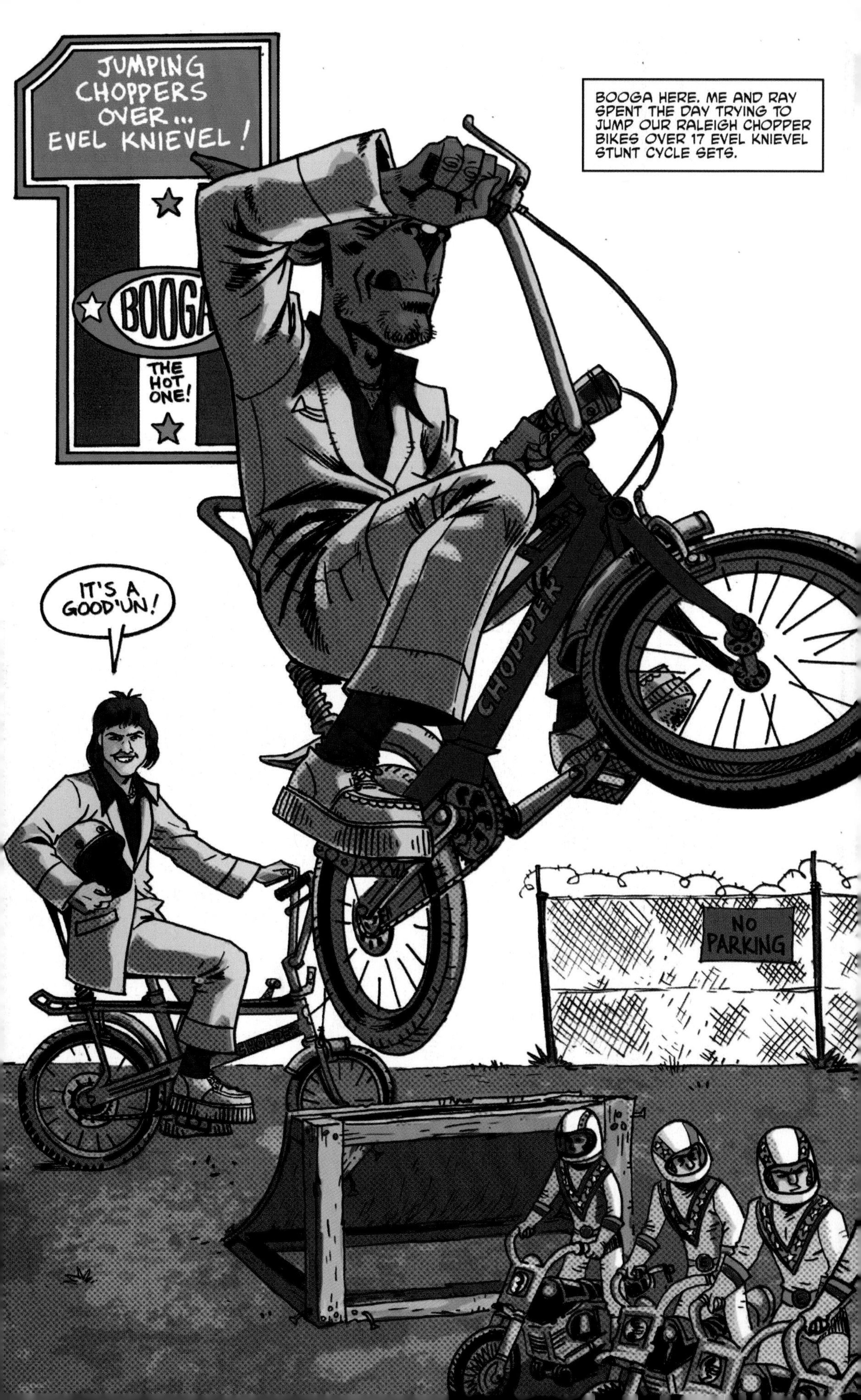
BOOGA HERE. ME AND RAY SPENT THE DAY TRYING TO JUMP OUR RALEIGH CHOPPER BIKES OVER 17 EVEL KNIEVEL STUNT CYCLE SETS.
JUMPING CHOPPERS OVER... EVEL KNIEVEL!
BOOGA
THE HOT ONE!
IT'S A GOOD'UN!
CHOPPER
NO PARKING

PUB LUNCH

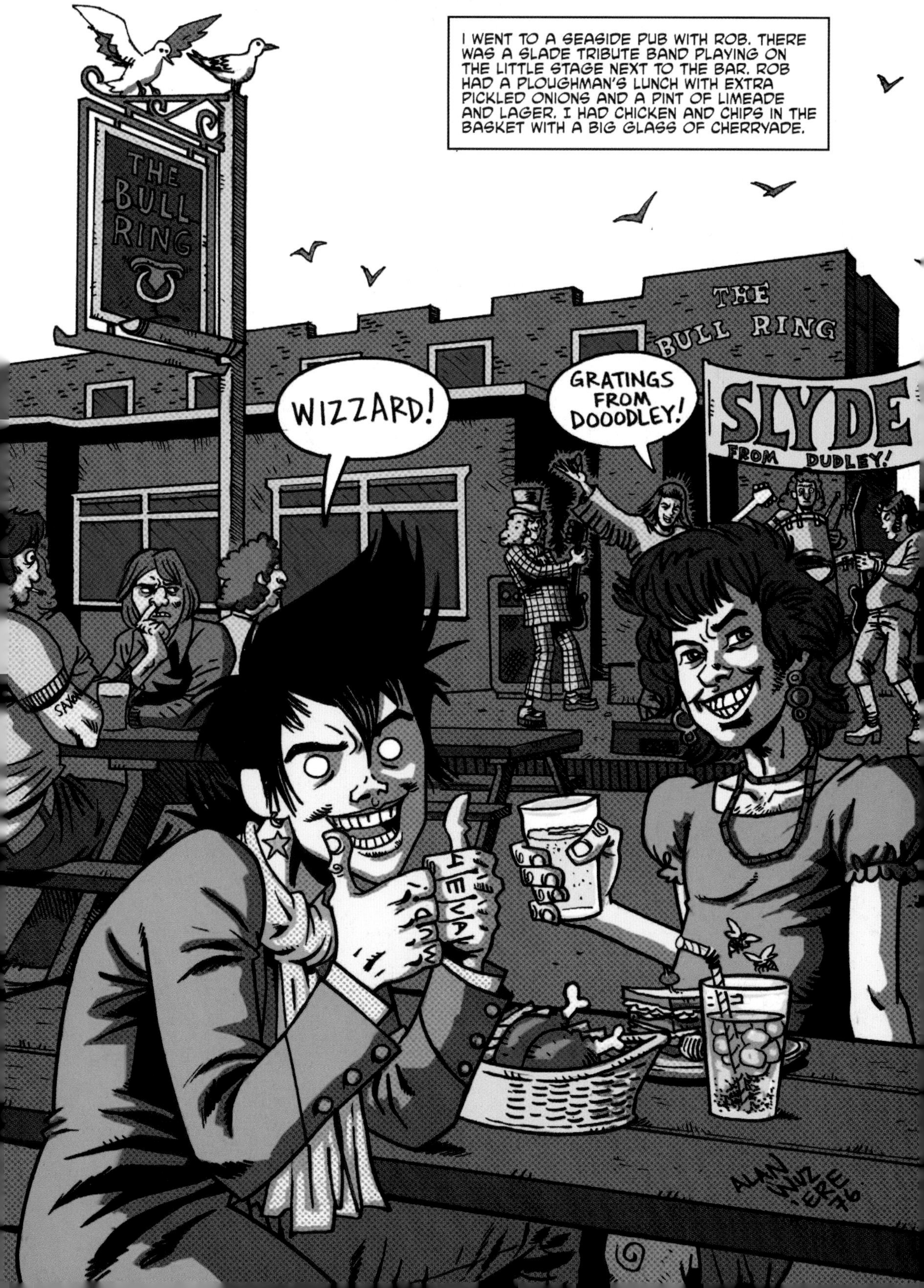
I WENT TO A SEASIDE PUB WITH ROB. THERE WAS A SLADE TRIBUTE BAND PLAYING ON THE LITTLE STAGE NEXT TO THE BAR. ROB HAD A PLOUGHMAN'S LUNCH WITH EXTRA PICKLED ONIONS AND A PINT OF LIMEADE AND LAGER. I HAD CHICKEN AND CHIPS IN THE BASKET WITH A BIG GLASS OF CHERRYADE.
THE BULL RING
THE BULL RING
SLYDE FROM DUDLEY!
WIZZARD!
GRATINGS FROM DOOODLEY!
4EVA
ALAN WUZ 'ERE '76

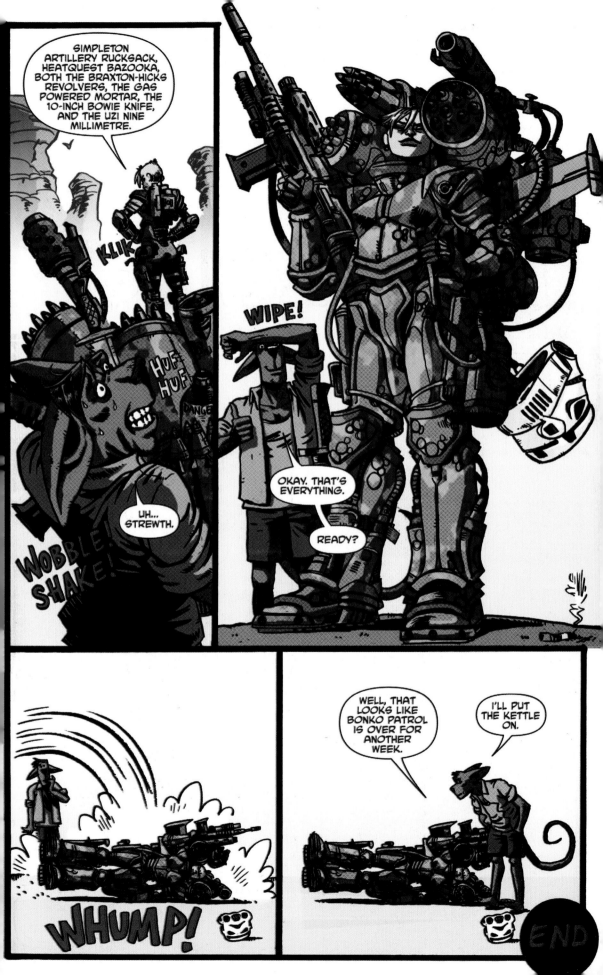

DIGGING THE LONELY ETERNITY

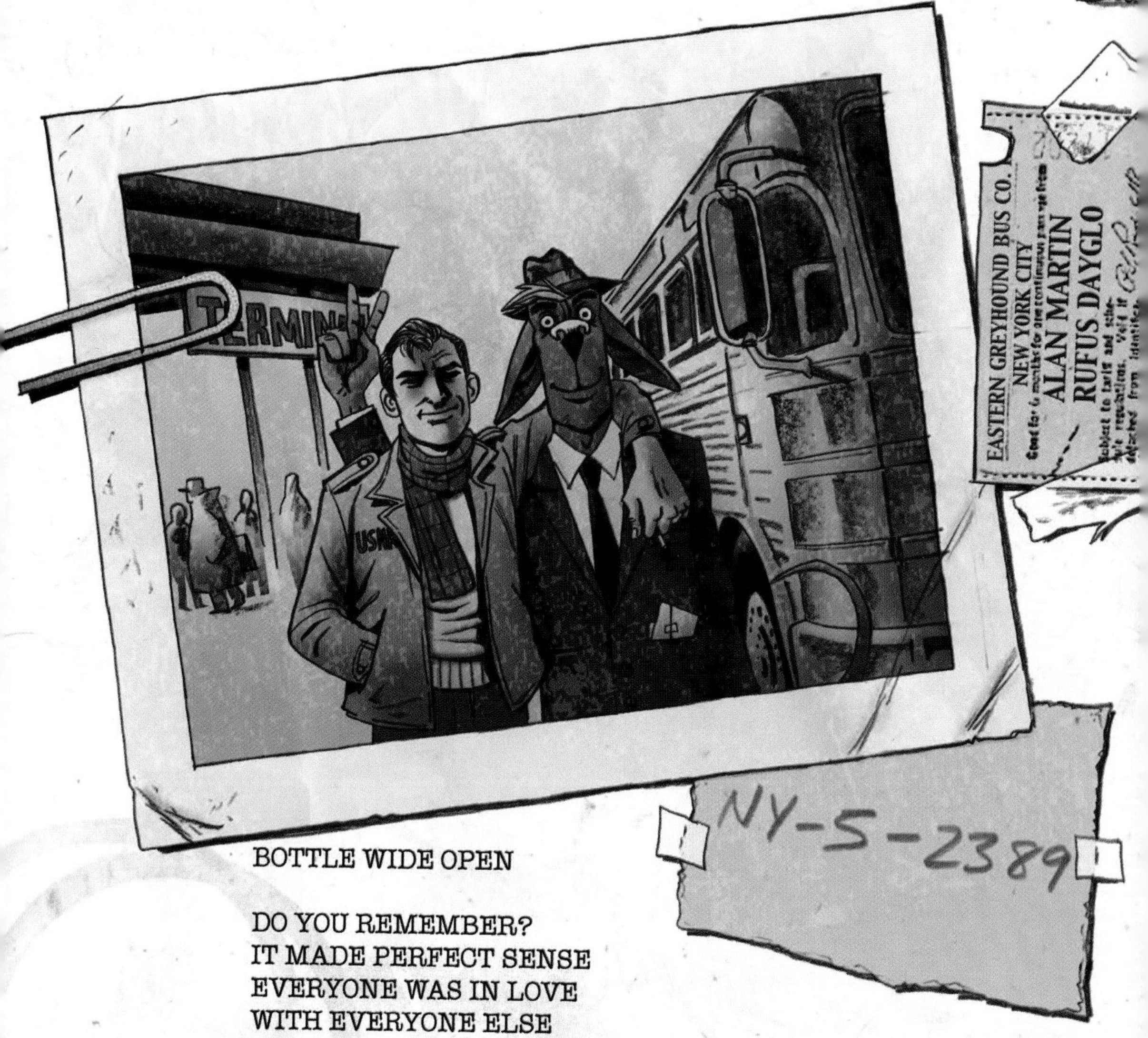
EASTERN GREYHOUND BUS CO.
NEW YORK CITY
ALAN MARTIN
RUFUS DAYGLO
NY-5-2389

BOTTLE WIDE OPEN

DO YOU REMEMBER?
IT MADE PERFECT SENSE
EVERYONE WAS IN LOVE
WITH EVERYONE ELSE
THE LIGHT SHONE DOWN
FROM THE EGG YOLK SUN
ONTO OUR STICKY BODIES
WE KISSED
AND PERSPIRED
ALL FOR ONE
AND ONE FOR ALL

HERE IT COMES AGAIN
I'VE CAPTURED IT IN A JAR
LIKE DUCHAMP'S BOTTLE OF PARIS AIR
I INTEND TO PULL OFF THE LID
AND FILL THE WORLD
WITH THE BEAUTY OF OUR HAPPY STENCH

STRAIGHT FROM THE BALLS

I'VE BEEN PUSHED
I'VE BEEN SHOVED
I'VE BEEN SHAT ON FROM ABOVE

I'VE BEEN BROKEN
LIKE A TOKEN
OF A LOVE THAT GOES UNSPOKEN

I'VE BEEN FOOLED
I'VE BEEN SWINDLED
MY POWER-PACK HAS DWINDLED

TRIED ESCAPE
FROM THIS SCHOOL
BASHED MY HEAD AGAINST THE WALL

I'M GIVING THIS TO YOU NOW

STRAIGHT FROM THE BALLS

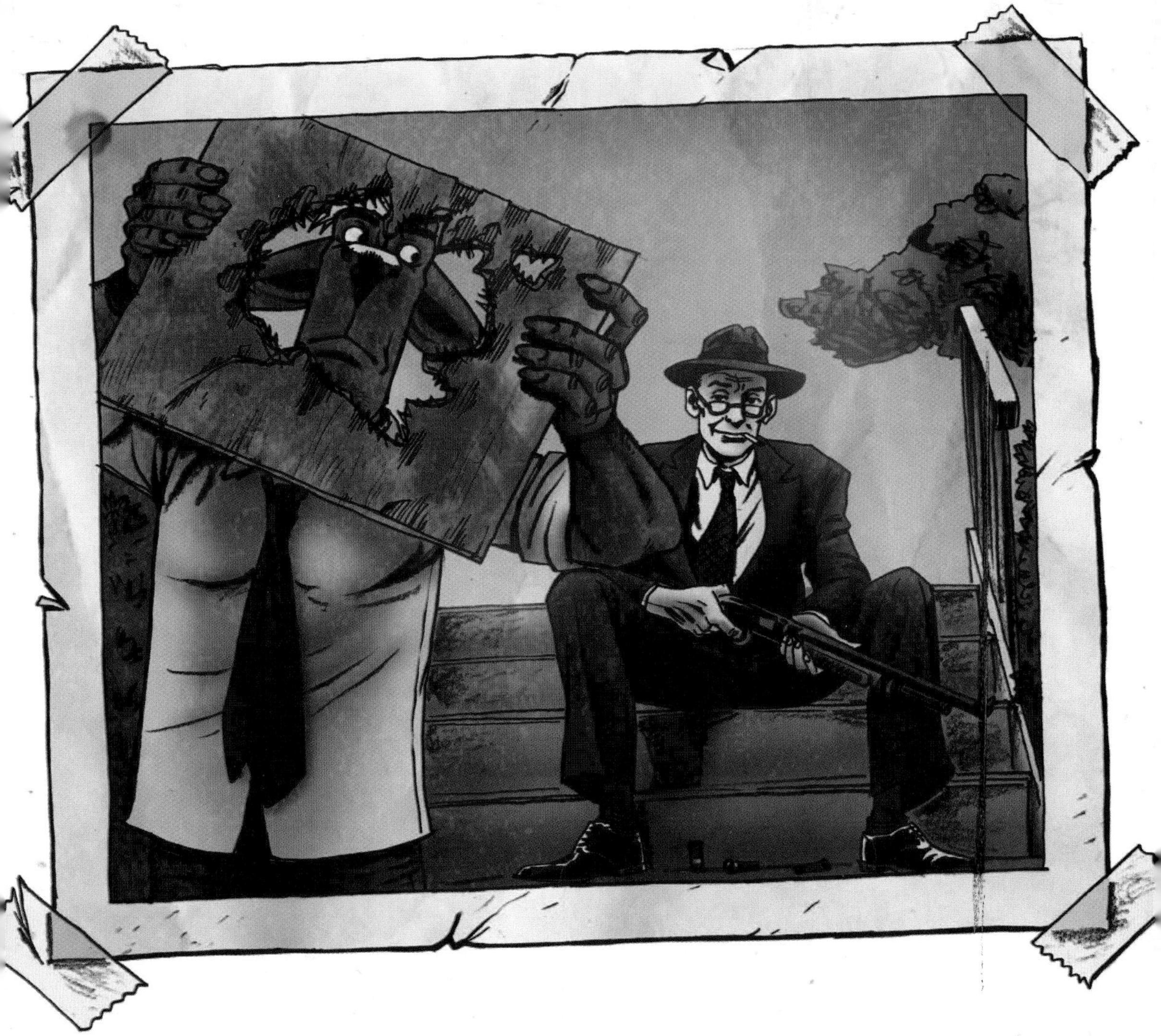

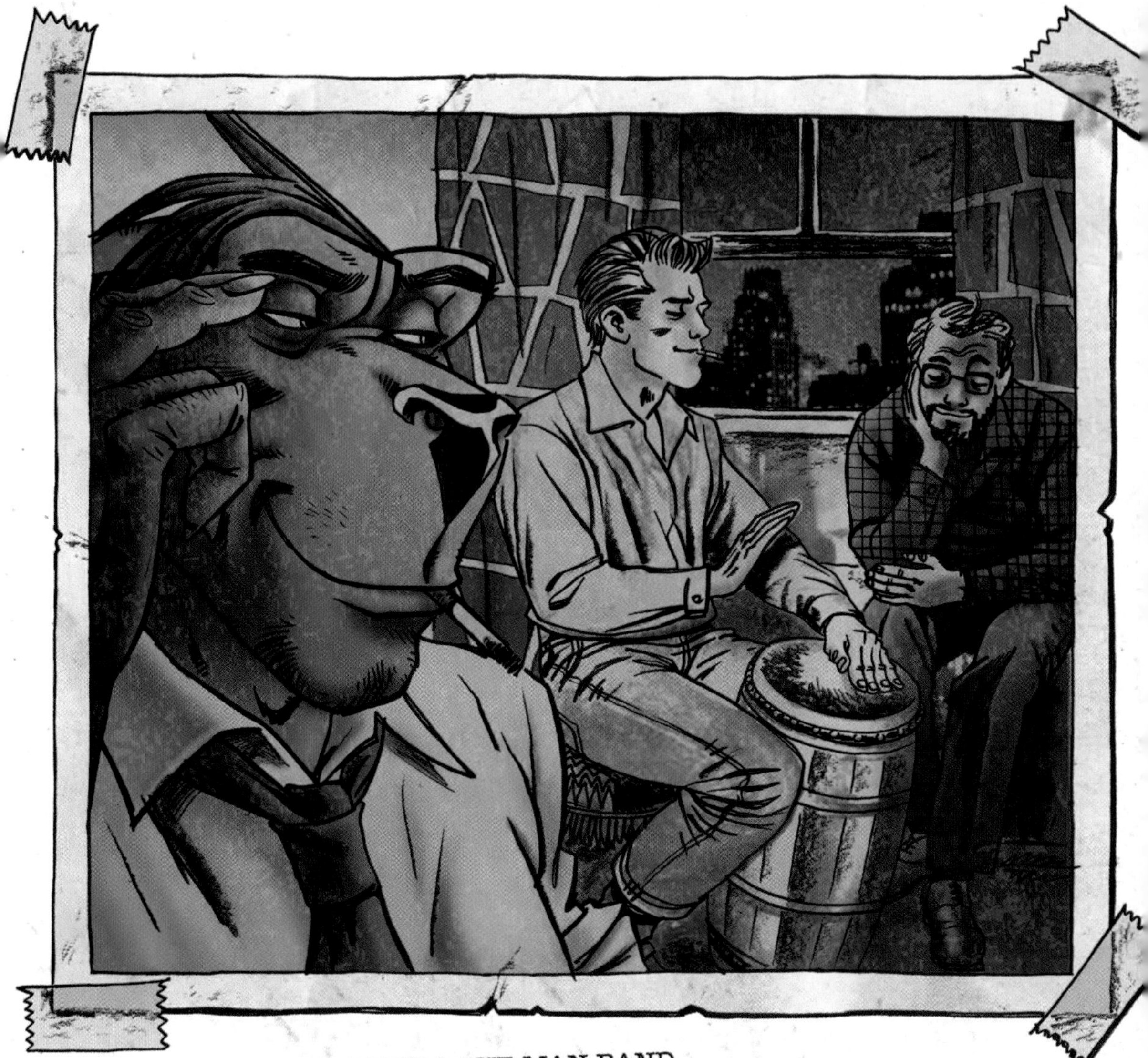

SUMMER IS A ONE-MAN-BAND

YOU'LL NEVER TRULY FIND YOURSELF
UNTIL YOU THE DAY YOU LOSE YOURSELF
ON A STREET WHERE YOU'VE NEVER BEEN
LEAVING YOUR SHOES ROUND SOMEONE'S HOUSE
SUCH A BLOODY HOT DAY
THE THIRST IN YOUR THROAT
CAN ONLY BE SATED
BY THE WORLD'S COLDEST BEER
IN THE WORLDS TALLEST GLASS
SERVED BY THE WORLD'S SWEETEST BARMAID
THE TWINKLE IN HER EYE
THE BRIGHTEST STAR IN THE SKY
ALPHA CENTAURI
JEANS COLLAPSE AROUND YOUR LEGS
FRAYING UNTO THE WIND
CRACKS APPEAR
IN THE DRY, DRY GROUND
YOUR ONE AND ONLY FRIEND

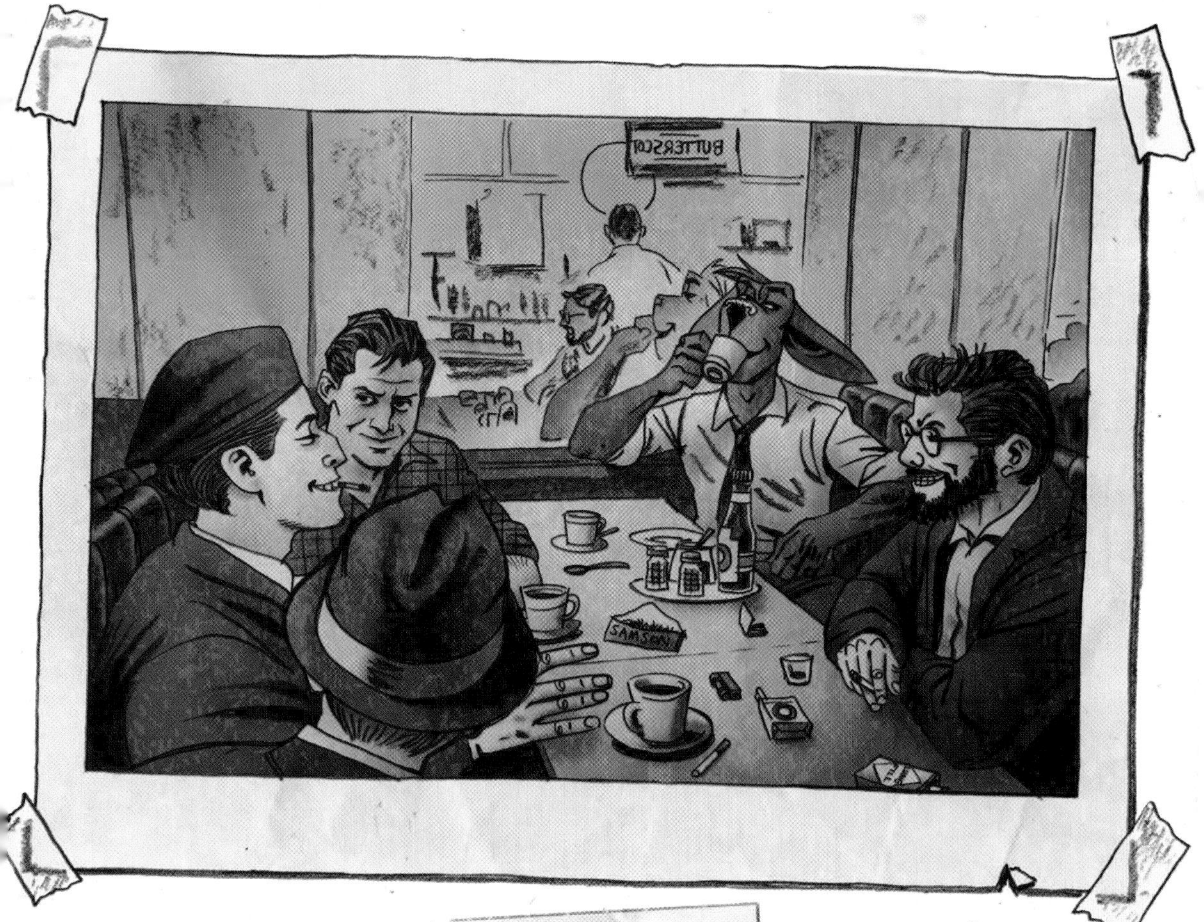
SAMSON

YOUR ORDER NUMBER
69

THE DEVIL AND THE DINOSAUR

THE DEVIL AND THE DINOSAUR
WERE OUT WALKING ON THE ROAD
SAID THE DEVIL TO THE DINOSAUR
"I'M GOING TO EXPLODE"

"NO PROBLEM" REPLIED THE DINOSAUR
"GO AHEAD AND BLOW UP RIGHT BY ME –
I'LL EXTINGUISH YOU IN AN INSTANT,
WITH A GIANT PREHISTORIC WEE"

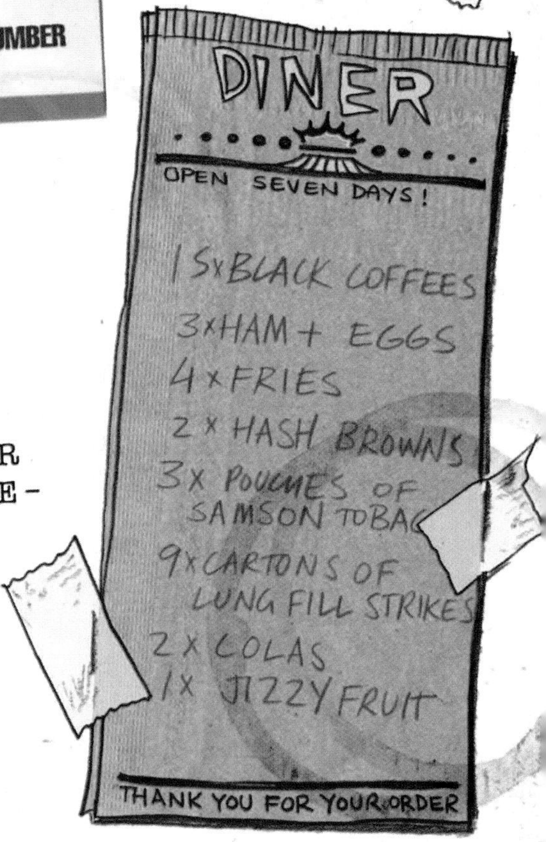
DINER
OPEN SEVEN DAYS!
15xBLACK COFFEES
3xHAM + EGGS
4xFRIES
2 x HASH BROWNS
3x POUCHES OF SAMSON TOBAC
9xCARTONS OF LUNG FILL STRIKES
2 x COLAS
1x JIZZY FRUIT
THANK YOU FOR YOUR ORDER

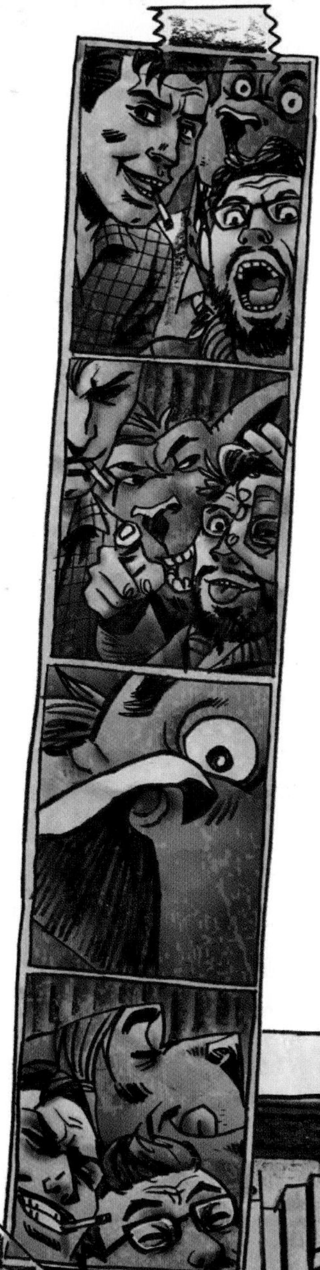

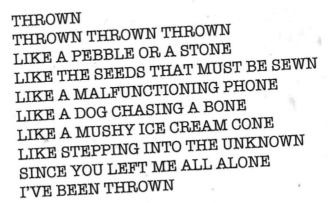

THROWN THROWN THROWN

THROWN
THROWN THROWN THROWN
LIKE A PEBBLE OR A STONE
LIKE THE SEEDS THAT MUST BE SEWN
LIKE A MALFUNCTIONING PHONE
LIKE A DOG CHASING A BONE
LIKE A MUSHY ICE CREAM CONE
LIKE STEPPING INTO THE UNKNOWN
SINCE YOU LEFT ME ALL ALONE
I'VE BEEN THROWN

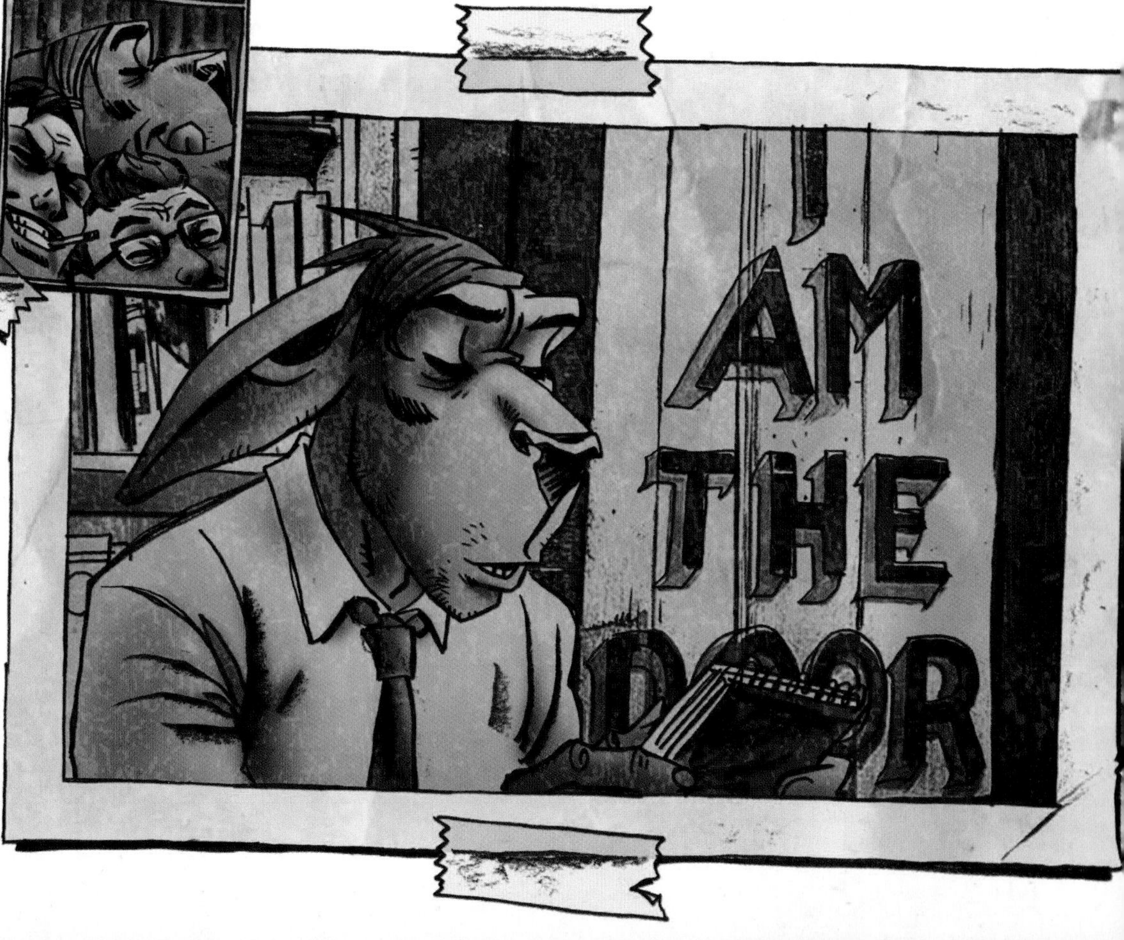
AM
THE
DOOR

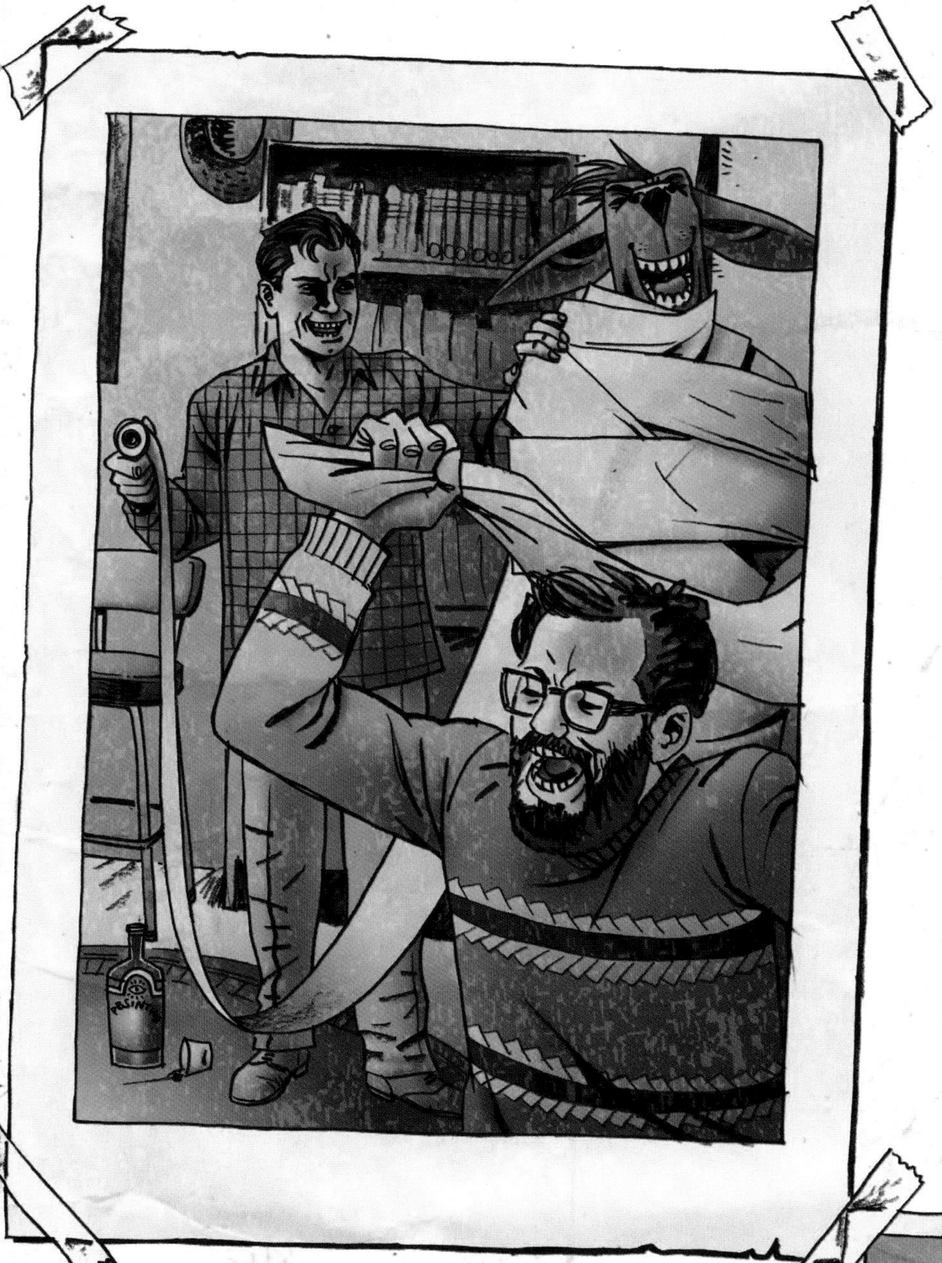

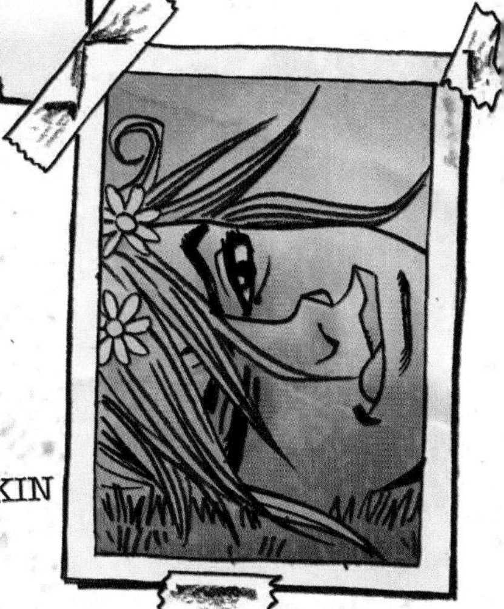

ON A ROLL

I USED A CONTINUOUS ROLL OF PAPER
TO GET MY IDEAS DOWN
TWELVE INCHES WIDE AND THIRTY FOOT LONG
TEN THOUSAND ADJECTIVES, VERBS AND NOUNS

I USED A TYPEWRITER AND A PENCIL
TO CONVERT MY SOUL INTO TEXT
IT DRIPPED FROM MY CHIN AND SEEPED OUT MY SKIN
THROUGH THE HOLES IN MY STRING VEST

I USED A ROLL OF TOILET PAPER
TO FINISH WHAT I HAD TO SAY
YOU READ IT IN ONE AND THEN WIPED YOUR BUM
AND YOU FLUSHED MY MEMORIES AWAY

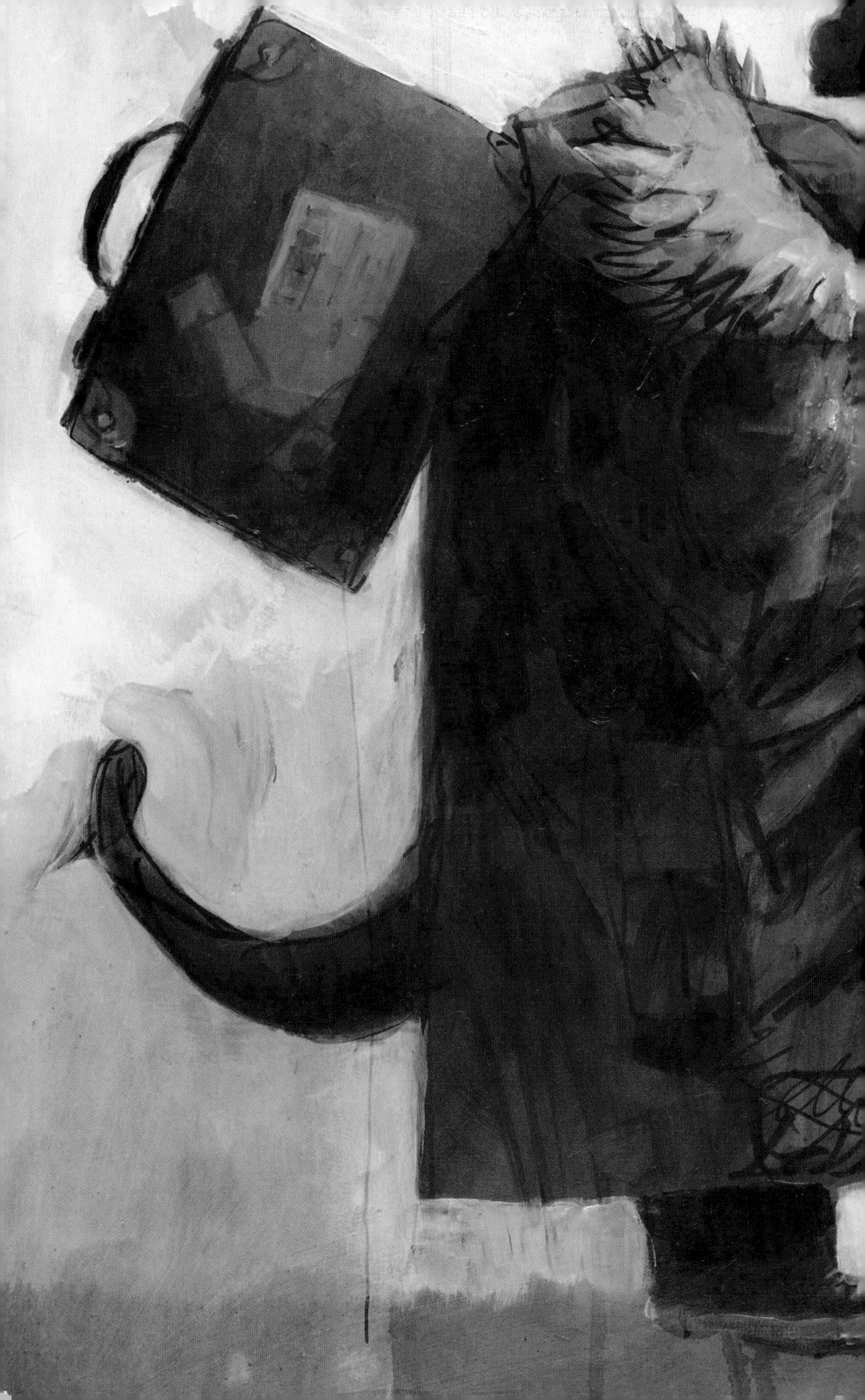

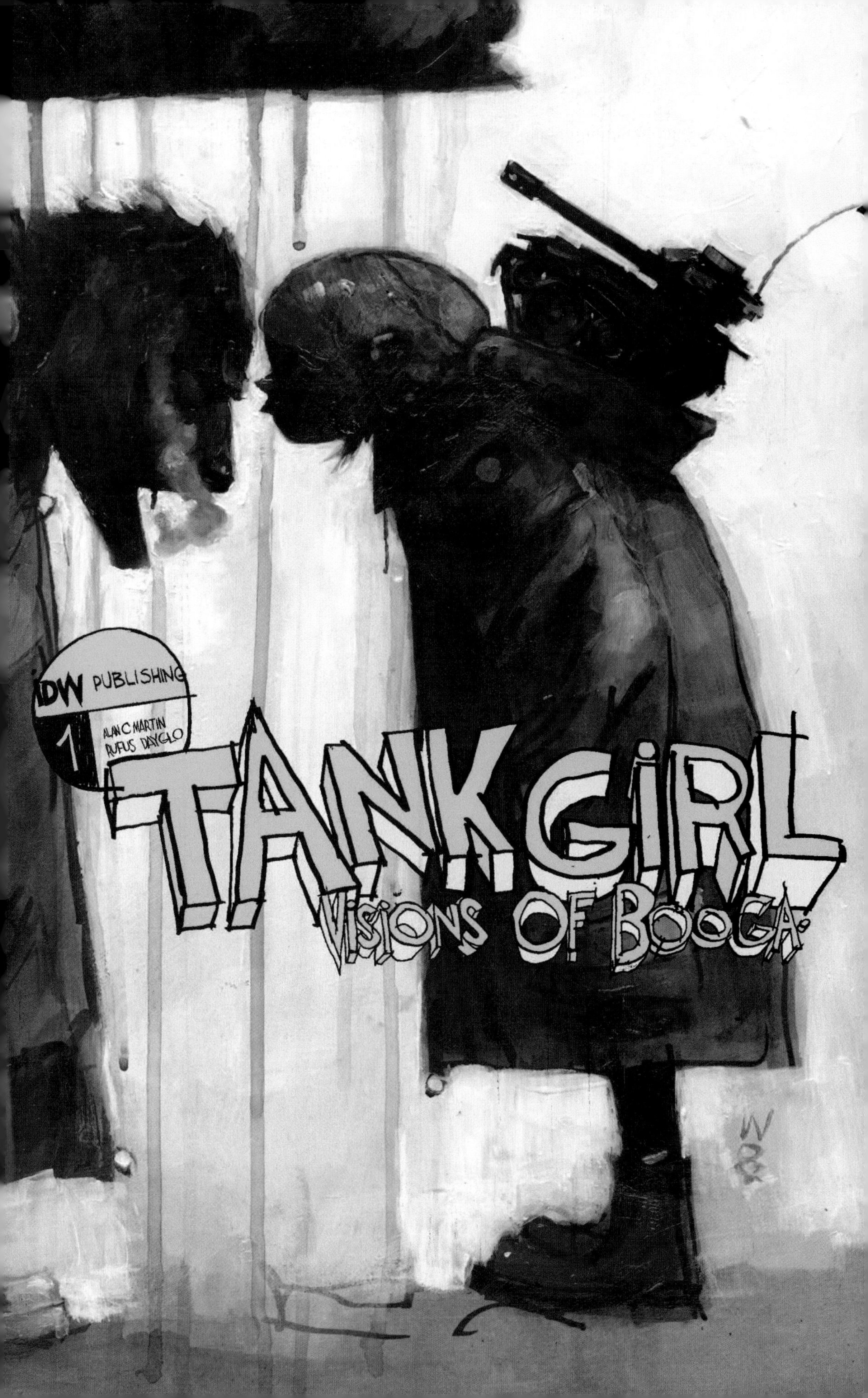
IDW PUBLISHING
1
ALAN C MARTIN
RUFUS DAYGLO
TANK GIRL
VISIONS OF BOOGA

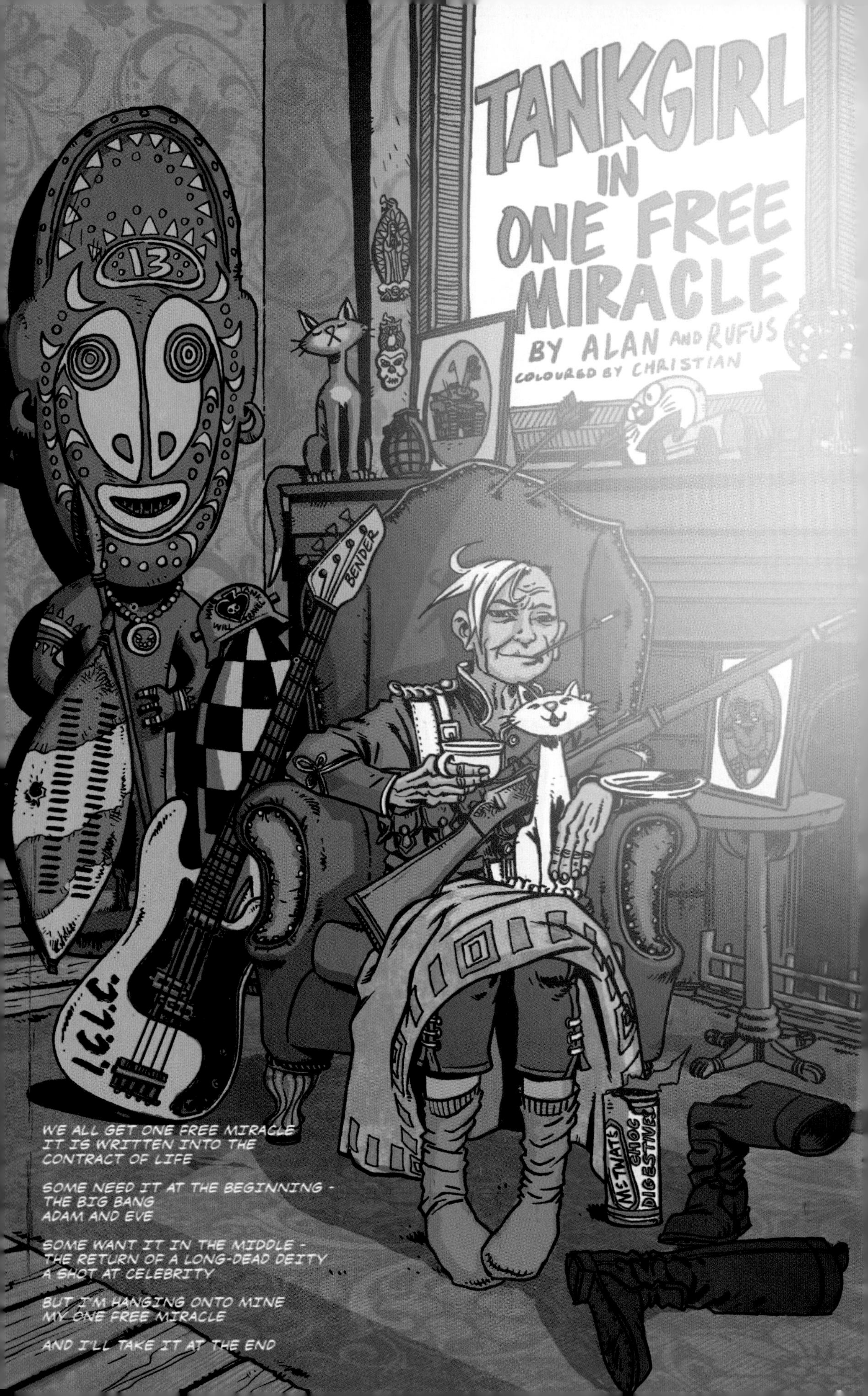
TANKGIRL
IN
ONE FREE
MIRACLE
BY ALAN AND RUFUS
COLOURED BY CHRISTIAN
13
BENDER
I.G.L.C.
MC TWATS CHOC DIGESTIVES
WE ALL GET ONE FREE MIRACLE
IT IS WRITTEN INTO THE
CONTRACT OF LIFE
SOME NEED IT AT THE BEGINNING -
THE BIG BANG
ADAM AND EVE
SOME WANT IT IN THE MIDDLE -
THE RETURN OF A LONG-DEAD DEITY
A SHOT AT CELEBRITY
BUT I'M HANGING ONTO MINE
MY ONE FREE MIRACLE
AND I'LL TAKE IT AT THE END